Top Heavy

Top Heavy

THE INCREASING
INEQUALITY
OF WEALTH IN AMERICA
AND WHAT
CAN BE DONE
ABOUT IT

An Expanded Edition
of a Twentieth Century
Fund Report

EDWARD N. WOLFF

THE NEW PRESS — NEW YORK

LIBRARY OF CONGRESS CATALOGING-IN-PUBLICATION DATA

Wolff, Edward N.
    Top Heavy: a study of the increasing inequality
    of wealth in America and what can be done about it/
    Edward N. Wolff.
    p. cm.
Includes bibliographical references and index.
ISBN 1-56584-347-9
    1. Wealth tax—United States. 2. Income distribution—
United States. I. Title.
HJ4120.W65   1996   96-23555
336.24'2—dc20   CIP

Top Heavy is an expanded edition of a Twentieth Century Fund study.
The Twentieth Century Fund sponsors and supervises timely analyses of economic policy,
foreign affairs, and domestic political issues. Not-for-profit and nonpartisan,
the Fund was founded in 1919 and endowed by Edward A. Filene.

Published in the United States by The New Press, New York
Distributed by W.W. Norton & Company, Inc., New York

*Established in 1990 as a major alternative to the large commercial publishing houses,
The New Press is a full-scale, nonprofit American book publisher outside
of the university presses. The Press is operated editorially in the public interest,
rather than for private gain; it is committed to publishing, in innovative ways, works
of educational, cultural, and community value that, despite their intellectual merits,
might not normally be commercially viable.
The New Press's editorial offices are located at the City University of New York.*

Production management by Kim Waymer
Printed in the United States of America

9 8 7 6 5 4 3 2 1

CONTENTS

FOREWORD

We Americans have always flattered ourselves that we have more of two good things than almost anyone else: democracy and opportunity. To be sure, neither is simple; the American ethos is not static, nor is it without contradictions. We reinvent ourselves through immigration; our democracy suffers low participation; our economy often seems to be in relative decline; our cities sometimes are viewed from the suburbs as if they were foreign nations. Still, in the past, the democratic foundation has held while economic opportunity has provided a glue that bound together America's oddly shaped parts.

Currently, there is a popular consensus that the nation is headed in the wrong direction. Public frustration and anger about representative democracy is acute. There also is a widespread belief that America offers less opportunity to today's young people than to past generations. Some blame international competition and immigration, some the education system, and some place responsibility upon government itself. Overall this frustration today seems to be shaking traditional American optimism.

Disquietingly, evidence supports the general conviction of diminished prospects for average citizens. Over the last several years, many studies have established that the working population of the United States—especially men with less than a college education—not only are doing more poorly than their parents, but that their real wages are declining. Between 1947 and 1973, American families in every income category enjoyed income growth—and the poorest families had the highest rate of all. Then, between 1973 and 1990, average income not only remained almost stagnant, but that average was a reflection of high income growth for the top 20 percent of families, and a significant fall in income for the poorest 20 percent. As a result, nearly half the families in the country have lower real income today than in 1973.

These issues were just reaching public awareness in January 1995, when the Twentieth Century Fund released the first edition of *Top Heavy* by Edward N. Wolff, a professor of economics at New York University. Wolff's report, the body of which is reprinted here with a postscript updating the material contained in the original, added data to our knowledge about trends in income distribution and provided analysis concerning wealth. While wealth inequality always has been—and continues to be—greater than income inequality, Wolff reported remarkable increases in wealth inequality. During the 1980s, the top 1 percent of wealth holders enjoyed two thirds of all increases in financial wealth. The bottom 80 percent of households ended up with less real financial wealth in 1989 than in 1983. Startlingly, Wolff reported that the United States had gone from a position of less wealth inequality among its citizens than in Europe to greater wealth inequality than is found in those class-ridden societies.

There was, notably, no good news in Wolff's research when it came to African-Americans. The median wealth of nonwhite citizens actually fell during the 1980s. It may be fashionable to look past such unpleasant information, but Wolff made an important contribution by simply forcing his readers to react to the eloquence of the facts.

From the facts, Wolff moved to policy. He offered a bold and carefully documented proposal to impose a wealth tax, similar to that in place in many European countries. Taking as his model the modest tax in effect in Switzerland, Wolff estimated that such a levy in the United States would produce about $40 billion, not much less than total excise tax collections. Under his proposal, even the wealthiest families would pay less than 10 percent of the annual real return on their capital as a new tax liability, and three-quarters of Americans would pay practically nothing.

Wolff's proposal confounded the (literally) "politically correct" notion that we must ignore growing inequality and exclude from consideration tax policy options that attempt to ameliorate the situation. But the Twentieth Century Fund believed that these were subjects worth discussing, if only to understand the forces that challenge democracy and economic opportunity. With a remarkably large segment of the population losing ground in wealth and income, the inevitably greater insecurity this group faces had to be considered a root cause of the anger shaking the democratic system.

Indeed, when the first edition of *Top Heavy* was released, Wolff's findings crystallized the growing interest in this issue and sparked a sharp and widespread controversy. Conservatives led the effort to discredit his work, holding fast to the notion that the years of the two Reagan administrations and the consequences of supply side economics involved a rising tide that had lifted all boats. But as increasing numbers of independent scholars came forth on Wolff's side of the argument, the weight of evidence and informed opinion essentially swamped the assertions of the critics. Put simply, Wolff's patient research and solid conclusions wound up convincing virtually all objective commentators.

In the postscript that updates his research in the light of newly available figures for the years 1989 to 1992, Wolff notes that slight shifts in wealth distribution have taken place (probably connected to the recession and sluggish stock market during that period). But, clearly, the overall picture remains about the same. Wealth inequality in America is still dramatic and persistent. And given the heavy concentration of stock ownership among the richest citizens, it is not unreasonable to speculate that the boom in the equity markets since 1992 suggests a further extension of the disturbing trends of the last two decades.

After twenty years, neither political rhetoric nor laissez-faire bromides have had any effect on this phenomenon. One thing, however, is clear: the problem keeps moving higher on the personal and public agenda of more and more Americans. Moreover, we are unlikely to have either the society or the economy we want until there is a reversal in the pattern of growing income and wealth inequality in the United States. Wolff's continuing work is important because it ensures that our understanding of these issues is grounded in dispassionate and rigorous analysis.

Thanks to The New Press, *Top Heavy* will continue to inform the ongoing debate about the state of the American economy. On behalf of the Trustees of the Twentieth Century Fund, I commend Professor Wolff and welcome the participation of The New Press.

RICHARD C. LEONE, PRESIDENT
The Twentieth Century Fund
June 1996

➤ 1

INTRODUCTION

Many people are aware that income inequality has increased over the past twenty years. Upper-income groups have continued to do well, decade after decade, while others, particularly those without a college degree, and especially the young, have seen their real income decline. The 1994 *Economic Report of the President* refers to the 1979–90 fall in real income of men with only four years of high school—a 21 percent decline—as "stunning."[1] Indeed, these changes in income distribution constitute one of the strongest arguments for the tax measures in President Clinton's 1993 deficit reduction program. Those at the top of the income distribution who are being asked to contribute more are the very people whose incomes grew most rapidly.

This paper broadens the discussion of distribution and taxation to include something that usually is neglected: wealth. Almost all discussions of distributional issues have centered on income. Income in any year is a measure of a household's economic position but it can vary greatly from year to year. A high income still can leave a household vulnerable. A better indicator of long-run economic security is wealth, the net worth of the household. Wealth is found by adding together the current value of all the assets a household owns—financial wealth such as bank accounts, stocks, bonds, life insurance savings, mutual fund shares; houses and unincorporated businesses; consumer durables like cars and major appliances; and the value of pension rights—and subtracting liabilities—consumer debt, mortgage balances, other outstanding debt. Wealth can vary from year to year as asset prices rise and fall, but it remains the foundation for a family's long-term security. Without wealth, a family lives from hand to mouth, no matter how high its income.

Examination of the data on wealth distribution leads to a disturbing question: Is America still the land of opportunity? The growing divergence evident in income distribution is even starker in wealth distribution. Equalizing trends of the 1930s–1970s reversed sharply in the 1980s. The gap between haves and have-nots is greater now than at any time since 1929. The sharp increase in inequality since the late 1970s has made wealth distribution in the United States more unequal than in what used to be perceived as the class-ridden societies of northwestern Europe.

Contrary to popular perception, the go-go years of the 1980s did not offer everyone a piece of the action. They were a party for those at the very top of the wealth distribution. While those in the fast lane enjoyed large increases in wealth during the 1980s, the wealth of the rest of the population did not simply grow more slowly; it actually fell. Looking at real financial wealth alone—including bank accounts, stocks, and bonds but excluding durable goods, housing, and pension wealth—80 percent of households experienced a decline between 1983 and 1989. Adding in housing wealth makes the picture somewhat less grim, but the bottom 40 percent of households still had less wealth in 1989 than in 1983.

Not surprisingly, in light of these facts, the racial distribution of wealth deteriorated in the 1980s from an already unacceptable level. Relative *income* of African American households held steady at about 60 percent of white income in the 1980s, but the relative *wealth* position of most black families deteriorated. Historically, black wealth always has been much lower than that of whites, the legacy of slavery, discrimination, and low incomes. Between 1983 and 1989, a bad situation grew worse. In 1983, the median white family had eleven times the wealth of the median nonwhite family. By 1989 this ratio had grown to twenty. Middle-class black households did succeed in narrowing the wealth gap with whites, but most nonwhite families moved even further behind. More than one in three nonwhite households now have no positive wealth at all, in contrast to one in eight white households.

These trends suggest that for reasons of fairness, the United States should consider broad taxation of wealth. Currently, we tax wealth in several specific ways. Our most important wealth tax, the property tax, is administered at the state and local level and is beyond the scope of this study. At the federal level, wealth is taxed through the capital gains tax and, at death, through estate taxes. Eleven other OECD countries have additional taxes on wealth. By studying these taxes and employing computer simulation, it is possible to assess the revenue effects and distributional implications that would be obtained were the tax systems of Germany, Sweden, or Switzerland to be adopted in the United States.

Although wealth taxation in one form or another is ubiquitous in rich countries, nowhere is it a major revenue source (that is, more than a small percentage of total revenue). The international mobility of financial wealth and widespread concern about the incentive effects of wealth taxation—incentives against saving and for capital flight—as well as the power of affluent elites all work to reduce the level of effective taxation. Nevertheless, even a very simple and modest tax like Switzerland's could raise substantial revenues in the United States. A wealth tax modeled on Switzerland's—with a $100,000 exclusion and a top rate for the wealthiest of three-tenths of one percent—would generate an estimated $40 billion annually. This is not much when measured against total federal revenues, to say nothing of total income or wealth. Nevertheless, it is significant in the context of the debates surrounding the Clinton budgets. A wealth tax offers us an important new fiscal option. It could be used to help finance any of the many needs of our society, from highway and bridge repair to environmental cleanup to health care to prisons. Or it could be used to replace other taxes that are deemed less fair or entail more damaging economic disincentives. And while any new tax would bring howls from the antitax lobby, given the concentration of financial wealth, it would be hard to find a lot of people who would be directly affected. Even the wealthiest households could be expected to pay less than 10 percent of the annual real return on their capital as their new wealth tax liability; more than three-quarters of all families would pay practically nothing. Would such a tax have terrible supply-side effects? Well, one might ask whether Switzerland suffers from capital flight and impoverishment.

➤ 2

WHY WEALTH?

Before exploring more closely the facts and policies surrounding wealth inequality, a review of the central concepts is helpful. Family *wealth* refers to the net dollar value of the stock of assets less liabilities (or debt) held by a household at one point in time.[1] *Income*, in contrast, refers to a flow of dollars over a period of time, usually a year. Though certain forms of income are derived from wealth, such as interest from savings accounts and bonds, dividends from stock shares, and rent from real estate, income and wealth are by no means identical. Many kinds of income—wages and salaries, food stamps and other transfer payments—are not derived from household wealth, and many forms of wealth, such as owner-occupied housing, produce no corresponding cash income flow.

Most people think of family income as a measure of well-being, but family wealth is also a source of well-being, independent of the direct income it provides. There are both narrowly economic and broader reasons for the importance of wealth. Some assets, particularly owner-occupied housing, provide services directly to their owner. This is also true for consumer durables, such as automobiles. Such assets can substitute for financial income in satisfying economic needs. Families receiving the same financial income but differing in their stocks of housing and consumer durables will experience different levels of well-being.

More important, perhaps, than its role as a source of income is the security that wealth brings to its owners, who know that their consumption can be sustained even if income fluctuates. Most assets can be sold for cash or used as collateral for loans, thus providing for unanticipated consumption needs. In times of economic stress, occasioned by such crises as unemployment, sickness, or family breakup, wealth is an important cushion. The very knowledge that wealth is at hand is a source of comfort for many families.

In the political arena, large fortunes can be a source of economic power and social influence that is not directly captured in the measure of annual income. Large accumulations of financial and business assets can confer special privileges on their holders. Such fortunes are often transmitted to succeeding generations, thus creating family "dynasties."

In most households, wealth varies from year to year. First, saving out of current income may augment wealth, just as spending in excess of income may diminish it. Second, assets already held by the family may change in value.[2] Finally, gifts and inheritances from or to a family member may change household wealth.

It is apparent that a family's wealth can be expected to depend on the age of its members because older working individuals generally will have spent more years saving and accumulating assets. Indeed, wealth, like income, is related to age, but the relationship is not a strong one since savings rates, the rate of return on asset holdings, and gifts and inheritances will generally differ among families of similar age profile, even when they have the same earnings history.

Wealth and income are positively correlated (that is, families with more income generally have more wealth), but this association, too, is far from perfect.[3] One reason is that rates of return on various components of wealth vary widely between years and within any one year.[4] Even well-reported asset and income data would yield an incomplete picture of the wealth from which they flow.[5] Other types of wealth, as noted above, may yield no income at all in a given year. Age explains part of the variation of the wealth-income ratio, but much is left unaccounted for.[6] As a result of this unexplained variability, wealth measures well-being differently from annual income, both in relative and absolute terms.

HOUSEHOLD WEALTH INEQUALITY IN THE UNITED STATES: PRESENT LEVEL AND HISTORICAL TRENDS

Wealth inequality in the United States was at a sixty-year high in 1989 (the latest date available), with the top 1 percent of wealth holders controlling 39 percent of total household wealth. Focusing more narrowly on financial wealth, the richest 1 percent of households owned 48 percent of the total. How did this come to pass? After the stock market crash of 1929, there ensued a gradual if somewhat erratic reduction in wealth inequality, which seems to have lasted until the late 1970s. Since then, inequality of wealth holdings, like that of income, has risen sharply (see Figure 3–1).[1] If Social Security and other pension wealth are included ("augmented wealth"), the improvement between 1929 and 1979 appears greater, but the increase in inequality since 1980 is still sharply in evidence.

The rise in wealth inequality from 1983 to 1989 (a period for which there is comparable detailed household survey information) is particularly striking. The share of the top 1 percent of wealth holders rose by 5 percentage points. The wealth of the bottom 40 percent showed an absolute decline. Almost all the absolute gains in real wealth accrued to the top 20 percent of wealth holders.

FIGURE 3–1
SHARE OF WEALTH OWNED BY THE TOP 1 PERCENT OF
HOUSEHOLDS IN THE UNITED STATES, 1922–1989

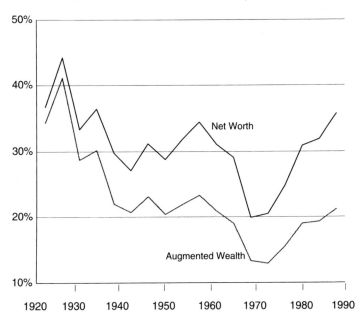

Source: Tabulations from Appendix, Table A–1, pages 62–63.

CHANGES IN AVERAGE WEALTH HOLDINGS

Look first at trends in real wealth over the period from 1962 to 1989 (all in 1989 dollars).[2] As Figure 3–2 shows, average wealth grew at a respectable pace from 1962 to 1983 and even faster thereafter. In fact, mean marketable wealth grew almost *twice as fast* between 1983 and 1989 as between 1962 and 1983 (3.4 percent per year vs. 1.8 percent). By 1989, the average wealth of households was $200,000, almost double that of 1962.

Average financial wealth grew faster than marketable wealth in the 1983–89 period (4.3 versus 3.4 percent per year), reflecting the increased importance of bank deposits, financial assets, and equities in the overall household portfolio over this period. This reversed the

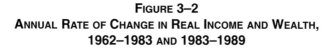

FIGURE 3–2
ANNUAL RATE OF CHANGE IN REAL INCOME AND WEALTH,
1962–1983 AND 1983–1989

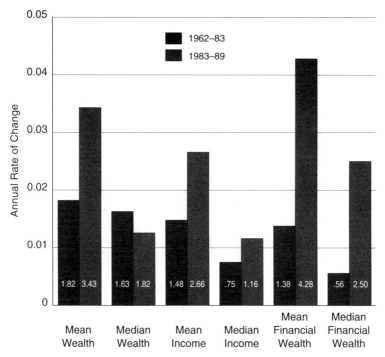

Source: 1962, from the Board of Governors of the Federal Reserve System, Survey of Financial Characteristics of Consumers; 1983, 1989 from the Board of Governors of the Federal Reserve System, Survey of Consumer Finances.

relationship of the 1962–83 period, when financial wealth grew more slowly than marketable wealth (1.4 versus 1.8 percent per year).

Average household income also grew faster in the 1983–89 period than in the 1962–83 period. Its annual growth accelerated from 1.5 percentage points to 2.7. However, in both periods average income grew more slowly than average wealth, with the difference rising from 0.3 percentage points per year for 1962–83 to 0.8 for 1983–89.

The robust growth of average wealth disguises some changes in the distribution of that wealth. This becomes clear after examination of *median* rather than *mean* wealth. Mean wealth is simply the average:

total wealth divided by total number of households. If the wealth of only the top 20 percent of households increases (with nothing else changing), then mean wealth increases because total wealth increases.[3] In contrast, the median of the wealth distribution is defined as the level of wealth that divides the population of households into two equal-sized groups (those with more wealth than the median and those with less). Returning to the earlier example, if only the top quintile enjoys an increase in wealth, median wealth is unaffected even though mean wealth increases because all additional wealth accrues to people well above the median income. The median tracks what is happening in the middle of the wealth distribution.[4] When trends in the mean deviate from trends in the median, this is a signal that gains and losses are unevenly distributed.

The trend in median household wealth in the United States gives a contrasting picture to the growth of mean wealth. Unlike mean marketable wealth, median marketable wealth grew faster in the 1962–83 period than in the later period (1.6 percent per year vs. 1.3 percent in 1983–89). Median wealth also grew much more slowly than mean wealth in the later period (a difference of 2.2 percentage points per year). Overall, from 1983 to 1989, while mean wealth increased by 23 percent, median wealth grew by only 8 percent. The fact that mean wealth grew much faster than median wealth after 1983 implies that the bulk of the gains were concentrated at the top of the distribution—a finding that implies rising wealth inequality.[5]

RISING WEALTH INEQUALITY IN THE 1980S

The rising level of wealth inequality between 1983 and 1989 is illustrated in Figure 3–3. The most telling finding is that the share of marketable net worth held by the top 1 percent, which had fallen by ten percentage points between 1945 and 1976, rose to 39 percent in 1989, compared with 34 percent in 1983.[6] Meanwhile, the share of wealth held by the bottom 80 percent fell by more than a fifth, from 19 to 15 percent.

These trends are mirrored in financial net worth, which is distributed even more unequally than total household wealth. In 1989, the top 1 percent of families as ranked by financial wealth owned 48 percent of the total (in contrast to 39 percent of total net worth). The top quintile accounted for 94 percent of total financial wealth, and the second quintile accounted for nearly all the remainder.

FIGURE 3–3

**PERCENTAGE SHARES OF TOTAL WEALTH AND INCOME
BY PERCENTILE GROUP IN 1983 AND 1989**

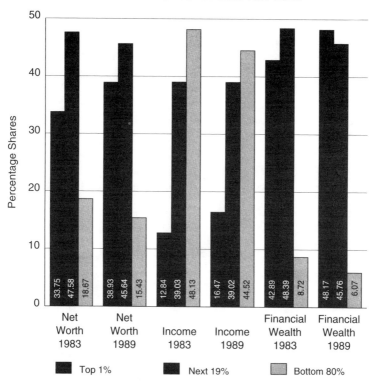

Source: 1983, 1989 are computations from the Survey of Consumer Finances .

The concentration of financial wealth increased to the same degree as that of marketable wealth between 1983 and 1989. The share of the top 1 percent of financial wealth holders increased by 5 percentage points, from 43 to 48 percent of total financial wealth. The share of the next 19 percent fell from 48 to 46 percent, while that of the bottom 80 percent declined from 9 to 6 percent.

Income distribution, too, became more concentrated between 1983 and 1989. As with wealth, most of the relative income gain accrued to the top 1 percent of recipients, whose share of total household income grew by 4 percentage points, from 13 to 17 percent.[7] The share of the next 19 percent remained unchanged at 39 percent. Almost all the (relative) loss in income was sustained by the bottom 80 percent of the income distribution, whose share fell from 48 to 45 percent.

Another way to view rising wealth concentration is to look at how the *increases* in total wealth were divided over a specified period. This is calculated by dividing the increase in wealth of each group by the total increase in household wealth.[8] The results, shown in Figure 3–4, indicate that the top 1 percent of wealth holders received 62 percent of the total gain in marketable wealth over the period from 1983 to 1989. The next 19 percent received 37 percent, while the bottom 80 percent

FIGURE 3–4
PERCENTAGE OF REAL WEALTH (INCOME) GROWTH
ACCRUING TO EACH PERCENTILE GROUP, 1983–1989

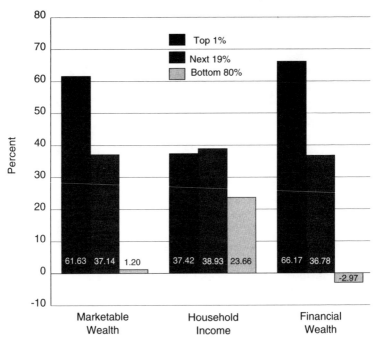

Source: 1983, 1989 are computations from the *Survey of Consumer Finances.*

received *only 1 percent*. This pattern represents a distinct turnaround from the 1962–83 period, when every group enjoyed some share of the overall wealth growth and the gains were roughly in proportion to the share of wealth held by each in 1962. Over this period, the top 1 percent received 34 percent of the wealth gains, the next 19 percent claimed 48 percent, and the bottom 80 percent got 18 percent.

Gains in the overall growth in financial wealth were distributed even more unevenly than in marketable net worth, with 66 percent of the growth accruing to the top 1 percent and 37 percent to the next 19 percent. The bottom 80 percent collectively lost 3 percent.

Finally, the changes in wealth distribution can be assessed by looking at the Gini coefficient. This indicator is used commonly to summarize data on the degree of inequality of income, wealth, or anything else of value. It ranges from 0 (exact equality) to 1 (one person owns everything); a higher Gini coefficient means greater inequality. This measure, like the others reviewed here, points to an increase in inequality: between 1983 and 1989 the Gini coefficient increased from 0.80 to 0.84.

The increase in wealth inequality recorded over the 1983–89 period in the United States is almost unprecedented. The only other period in the twentieth century during which concentration of household wealth rose comparably was from 1922 to 1929. Then inequality was buoyed primarily by the excessive increase in stock values, which eventually crashed in 1929, leading to the Great Depression of the 1930s.

➤ 4

THE CHANGING STRUCTURE
OF HOUSEHOLD WEALTH

In order to assess the likely incidence of wealth taxation in the United States—who is likely to pay and how much—it is necessary to analyze the variation of household wealth by demographic group and the composition of wealth. There are substantial differences in wealth holding by demographic category. Households in the age group 45–69[1] are by far the wealthiest group in our country, with those 70 and over in second place and households under 45 a distant third. Between 1983 and 1989 the two less privileged age cohorts made gains in relative wealth holdings. Over the same period, white and nonwhite households' mean wealth continued to converge. Nevertheless, the gap in mean wealth holdings between whites and nonwhites remained very large in comparison with income differences (a ratio of 0.29 for wealth versus 0.63 for income). Moreover, the lower half of the distribution for nonwhite households actually fell further behind the lower half for white households (median wealth diverged), hinting that wealth inequality among nonwhites has been growing even faster than among the population at large.

WEALTH HOLDINGS BY AGE GROUP

One key predictor for differences in wealth among families is age. Individuals typically accumulate wealth until retirement age; thereafter, they spend down their savings.[2] Figure 4–1 confirms this pattern.

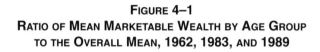

FIGURE 4–1
RATIO OF MEAN MARKETABLE WEALTH BY AGE GROUP
TO THE OVERALL MEAN, 1962, 1983, AND 1989

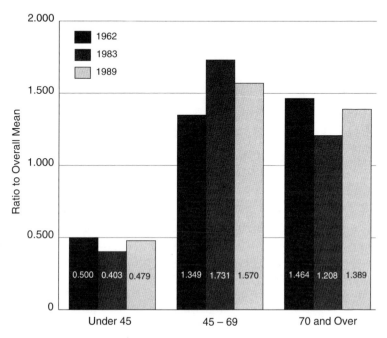

Source: 1962, from the *Survey of Financial Characteristics of Consumers* ; 1983, 1989 from the *Survey of Consumer Finances.*

In 1983, the average marketable wealth of families under the age of forty-five was far below the overall average, while that of families over forty-five was well above the average, though less so in the case of elderly households. "Hump-shaped" profiles are also found for 1962 and 1989.

Despite the overall similarity in the three age-wealth profiles, there have been notable shifts in relative wealth holdings. Between 1962 and 1983, middle-aged households gained at the expense of both the younger and older households. The wealth of families under forty-five declined from 50 percent of average to 40 percent, that of the middle-aged increased from 135 to 173 percent of average, and that of the older group fell from 146 to 121 percent of the average.

The years 1983 to 1989 saw an exact reversal of this pattern. The wealth of families under forty-five increased from 40 percent of the overall mean in 1983 to 48 percent in 1989, close to the corresponding 1962 figure. The relative wealth of the middle-aged fell from 173 percent of average in 1983 to 159 in 1989, still above the comparable 1962 figure. The wealth holdings of older households grew from 121 percent in 1983 to 139 percent in 1989, remaining below their corresponding level in 1962.

RACIAL DIFFERENCES IN HOUSEHOLD WEALTH

On the basis of the *Current Population Reports*, the relative gap in income between nonwhite and white households was almost identical in 1967 and 1989 (see Table 4–1). The ratio of mean household income remained at 0.63, and the ratio of median income held at slightly below 0.6. The story of household wealth is more discouraging. From 1983 to 1989 the ratio of mean wealth increased (from 0.24 to 0.29), but the ratio of median wealth fell from the already shockingly low level of 0.09 to only 0.05, leading to the inference that most of the gains for nonwhite households were captured by the upper half of the distribution rather than those less well off.

Notably, the home ownership rate based on decennial census data almost doubled among nonwhite families between 1940 and 1980 (from 24 percent to 44 percent). Indeed, the ratio of home ownership rates between nonwhites and whites increased from 52 percent in 1940 to 64 percent in 1985. However, these increases were confined to the 1940s and the 1960s. Since 1970, there has been no increase in the home ownership rate among nonwhite families. According to the *Survey of Consumer Finances* (SCF) data, it actually fell slightly between 1983 and 1989, from 43.6 to 43.3 percent.

Turning to wealth more broadly defined, one finds that nonwhite families also made substantial gains on whites in terms of both mean and median net worth between the early 1960s and the early 1980s. According to the SCF data, the gap in mean wealth closed further during the 1980s. Yet the gap in median wealth widened. This result reflects a greater inequality in wealth among nonwhites than whites. In 1989, for example, 35 percent of nonwhite families reported zero or negative net worth, compared to 12 percent of whites. Thus, though there have been some gains in closing the racial wealth gap among better-off nonwhites, the differential is large and growing for the median family.

Table 4–1
Ratio of Household Income and Wealth and Homeownership
Rates Between Nonwhites and Whites, 1940–1989

	Ratio of	
Year	Means	Medians

I. Household Income[a]

Year	Means	Medians
1967	0.63	0.58
1983	0.62	0.57
1989	0.63	0.59

[a] Results based on U.S. Bureau of the Census, *Current Population Reports* (Washington, D.C.: Government Printing Office, 1990), Table 2, pp. 21–22. Ratio is between black and white households; Hispanic households are excluded from this table.

II. Homeownership Rates[b]

Year	Means
1940	0.52
1950	0.61
1960	0.60
1970	0.64
1980	0.65
1985	0.64

[b] Calculations based on decennial census data from the U.S. Bureau of the Census (1989), p. 706. Ratio is between whites and nonwhites. Hispanic families may be classified in either group.

III. Net Worth[c]

Year	Means	Medians
1962	0.12	0.04
1983	0.24	0.09
1989	0.29	0.05

[c] Compilations from the *Survey of Financial Characteristics of Consumers* (1962); *Survey of Consumer Finances* (1983 and 1989). Hispanics are classified as nonwhites in 1983 and 1989.

THE COMPOSITION OF WEALTH

The portfolio composition of household wealth shows the forms in which households save. Do households save for direct consumption, as in acquiring ownership of houses and automobiles? Do families save for precautionary reasons, as in the form of bank deposits? Do they save for retirement, as in insurance plans, IRAs (individual retirement accounts), or the like? Or do they save mainly for investment purposes, as in financial securities and corporate stock?

Overall, between 1962 and 1989 there was a major shift in household portfolios out of financial assets and equities (deposits, bonds, stocks, and trusts), which declined from 52 percent of gross wealth to 38 percent, and a corresponding increase in real estate and unincorporated business equity, rising from 48 percent to 59 percent. Debt as a proportion of net worth, after falling from 16.4 to 15.1 percent between 1962 and 1983, increased to 16.5 percent in 1989.

Many people believe that housing (more specifically, owner-occupied housing) is by far the most important asset the household controls. Owner-occupied housing was indeed the most important asset in the household portfolio in 1962, 1983, and 1989 (see Figure 4–2). However, in none of the three years was its gross value more than a third of total assets, or its net value more than one-quarter. In 1989, housing accounted for 29 percent of the gross value of assets, and net equity in owner-occupied housing—the value of the house minus any outstanding mortgage—was only 20 percent of gross assets (or 24.9 percent of net worth). Checking deposits, savings accounts (including money market funds), and other deposits (including retirement plans like IRAs)[3] amounted to 17 percent. Real estate other than owner-occupied housing and unincorporated business equity comprised 29 percent of total assets. Corporate stock, bonds and other financial securities, and trust equity amounted to 21 percent. Debt as a proportion of gross assets was 14 percent.

There have been some significant changes in the composition of household wealth since 1962. Popular perception is that housing is the only substantial asset that most families can claim, but figures show this is increasingly untrue. The gross value of housing as a proportion of gross assets increased from 26 percent in 1962 to 30 percent in 1983 but then declined slightly to 29 percent in 1989.[4] Other (nonhome) real

FIGURE 4–2
COMPOSITION OF HOUSEHOLD WEALTH
(PERCENTAGE OF GROSS ASSETS, 1962, 1983, AND 1989)

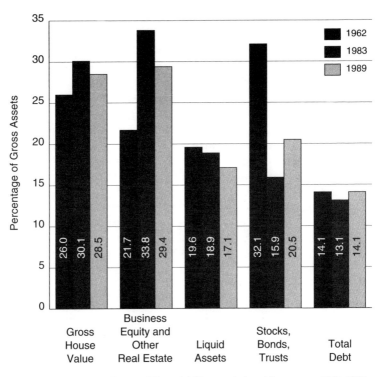

Source: 1962, from the Survey of Financial Characteristics of Consumers; 1983, 1989 from the Survey of Consumer Finances.

estate and business equity grew rapidly between 1962 and 1989, from 22 to 29 percent of total assets. Liquid assets, including checking and savings accounts, money market funds, CDs, life insurance, and pension accounts, remained relatively steady at 20 and 19 percent of total assets in 1962 and 1983, respectively, falling to 17 percent in 1989. Financial securities (bonds), corporate stock, and trust equity declined in importance in the household portfolio from 32 percent in 1962 to 16 percent in 1983, and then increased during the latter part of the 1980s to 21 percent in 1989.

➤ 5

COMPARISONS WITH OTHER COUNTRIES

Due to differences in reference sources, definitions of household wealth, and accounting conventions, international comparisons of household wealth inequality must be made cautiously. However, the evidence seems to suggest that in the early part of this century, (the 1920s are the earliest period for which data are available), wealth inequality was much lower in the United States than in the United Kingdom, while U.S. figures were comparable to Sweden. America appeared to be the land of opportunity, whereas Europe was a place where an entrenched upper class controlled the bulk of wealth. By the late 1980s, the situation appears to have completely reversed, with much higher concentration of wealth in the United States than in Europe. Europe now appears the land of equality.

UNITED KINGDOM AND SWEDEN. There are two other countries besides the United States for which long-term time-series are available on household wealth inequality: the United Kingdom and Sweden. The most comprehensive data exist for the United Kingdom. The data are based on estate duty (tax) return data and, as a result, use mortality multipliers to obtain estimates of the wealth of the living (see Appendix for methodology). Estimates are for the adult population (that is, individuals, not households). Figures are available on an almost continuous basis from 1923 to 1990.[1]

The Swedish data are available on a rather intermittent basis from 1920 through 1990. The data are based on actual wealth tax returns. Tax return data are subject to error, like other sources of wealth data. The principal problem is underreporting owing to tax evasion and legal tax exemptions. However, some assets, such as housing and stock shares, are extremely well covered because of legal registration requirements in Sweden. Also, the deductibility of interest payments from taxable income makes it likely that the debt information is very reliable. On the other hand, bank accounts and bonds are not subject to similar tax controls, and it is likely that their amounts are underreported.

Figure 5–1 shows comparative trends among the three countries.[2] For the United Kingdom, there was a dramatic decline in the degree of individual wealth inequality from 1923 to 1974 but little change thereafter. Based on a conventional definition of wealth (marketable wealth), the share of the top 1 percent of wealth holders fell from 59 percent in 1923 to 20 percent in 1974. However, between 1974 and 1990, there was only a relatively minor reduction in the concentration of household wealth, as the top percentile saw their share shrink to 18 percent.

In Sweden, as in the United Kingdom, there was a dramatic reduction in wealth inequality between 1920 and the mid-1970s. Based on the years for which data are available, the decline appears to have been a continuous process. Over this period, the share of the top percentile declined from 40 percent to 17 percent of total household marketable wealth. Between 1975 and 1985, there was virtually no change in the concentration of wealth. However, this was followed by a sharp increase in wealth inequality between 1985 and 1990, with the share of the top percentile increasing to 21 percent, a level similar to that of the early 1960s.

Comparisons among the three countries are instructive. In all three countries, there was a fairly sizable reduction in wealth concentration until the late 1970s, though the pattern was much more cyclical in the United States than in the other two. However, during the 1980s, both the United States and Sweden showed a rather sharp increase in wealth inequality, whereas the trend was almost flat in the United Kingdom. This is a surprising difference, since both the United States (under Ronald Reagan) and the United Kingdom (under Margaret Thatcher) pursued conservative economic policies while the Social Democrats dominated in Sweden. Moreover, of the three countries, Sweden is the only one with a direct tax on household wealth. This suggests that differences in public policy alone cannot account for these trends in wealth distribution.

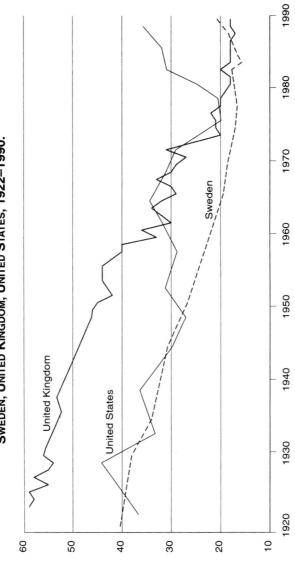

FIGURE 5–1

SHARE OF MARKETABLE NET WORTH HELD BY TOP 1 PERCENT OF WEALTH HOLDERS: SWEDEN, UNITED KINGDOM, UNITED STATES, 1922–1990.

Source: U.S. data from Appendix, Table A–1; U.K. data from Shorrocks (1987) and Board of Inland Revenue (1992), series c; data for Sweden from Spånt (1987) and Statistics Sweden (1992).

FRANCE/UNITED STATES COMPARISON. Because of the difficulties of comparing wealth data from different countries, a special study was undertaken to compare the distribution of household wealth in France and the United States.[3] The main difficulty in the study was that survey data in the two countries cover different assets and liabilities (in fact, the French survey did not include any information on household debt). In order to compare the two distributions, it was necessary to create a "conformable" set of balance sheet accounts for the two countries.

Table 5–1 shows comparative data for the size distribution of house-hold gross wealth in the two countries.[4] For gross assets in France, the share of the top 1 percent is 26 percent of the total, and that of the top quintile is 69 percent; the overall Gini coefficient is 0.71. The shares of the top 1, 5, and 20 percent are considerably higher in the United States than in France, whereas the share of the second quintile is substantially higher in France. The shares of the bottom three quintiles are similar in the two countries. On the basis of the original U.S. data adjusted to the French concept of wealth, the American Gini coefficient is 0.77, considerably higher (more unequal) than the French.

The results indicate that wealth is more unequally distributed in the United States than in France. The differences are considerable. This result is also consistent with the finding that French households keep a substantially higher proportion of their wealth in the form of owner-occupied housing, which is more equally distributed among the population than most other assets (particularly bonds and corporate stock).[5]

Weighing the evidence leads to the judgment that wealth inequality in the United States is high by international standards. It appears to be higher than in France and, despite the differences in sources and methods, higher than in Sweden and the United Kingdom during the postwar period, particularly since 1980. This result is perhaps not too surprising, since many studies have shown that recent income inequality is greater as well in the United States than in most other industrialized economies.[6] This finding represents a turnaround from the early part of the century, when inequality in household wealth appeared to be much larger in European countries such as the United Kingdom and Sweden than in the United States.

TABLE 5–1

SIZE DISTRIBUTION OF GROSS HOUSEHOLD ASSETS
IN FRANCE (1986) AND THE UNITED STATES (1983)[a]

	GINI COEFF.	PERCENTAGE OF TOTAL ASSETS HELD BY:						
		TOP 1%	TOP 5%	TOP QUINT.	2ND QUINT.	3RD QUINT.	4TH QUINT.	BOT. QUINT.
A. *France, 1986*	.71	26	43	69	19	9	2	1
B. *United States, 1983*								
1. Original Survey Data	.77	33	54	78	14	7	2	0
2. Survey Data Aligned to National Balance Sheet Totals[b]	.73	30	51	75	14	7	4	1

[a] The U.S. data use the same wealth concept as the French data.

[b] Line 2 shows the results of the alignment of the U.S. data with national balance sheet totals. Measured inequality falls by all indices, mainly due to the substantial upward adjustment of the value of demand deposits, time deposits, and insurance savings. However, wealth inequality in the United States is still greater than in France, though the differences are not as pronounced. It should be stressed that a similar exercise on the French data could have lowered measured wealth inequality in France to a similar degree.

Source: Kessler and Wolff (1991).

COMPARISONS WITH INCOME INEQUALITY

Wealth inequality is today and has always been extreme and substantially greater than income inequality. Indeed, the top 1 percent of wealth holders has typically held in excess of one-quarter of total household wealth, in comparison to the 8 or 9 percent share of income received by the top percentile of the income distribution. Figure 6–1 shows the historical pattern of wealth and income inequality through means of the shares held by the most prosperous families.[1]

Thirty-seven percent of the total real income gain between 1983 and 1989 accrued to the top 1 percent of income recipients (in contrast to 62 percent of the marketable wealth gain), 39 percent went to the next 19 percent of the income distribution, and 24 percent accrued to the bottom 80 percent (versus only 1 percent of the marketable wealth gain). While not as powerfully as in the case of wealth, these results for income show again that the growth in the economy during the 1980s was concentrated in a surprisingly small part of the population. To put it succinctly, the top quintile received more than three-quarters of the total increase in income and essentially *all* of the increase in wealth. The starkness of these numbers suggests a widening fissure seaprating the strata within our society.

Though wealth is more unequally distributed, the historical course of wealth distribution has roughly paralleled that of income distribution.

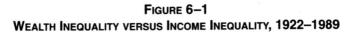

FIGURE 6–1
WEALTH INEQUALITY VERSUS INCOME INEQUALITY, 1922–1989

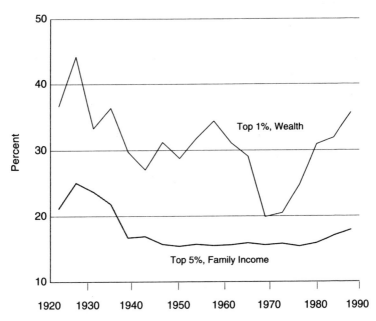

Source: Data from Appendix, Table A–1; Kuznets (1953); U.S. Bureau of the Census, *Current Population Reports* (1991).

Income inequality, as measured by the share flowing to the top 5 percent, increased between 1922 and 1929—from 21.2 to 25.1 percent—declined steadily during the depression years—reaching a 21.8 percent share in 1939—and then fell precipitously during World War II. There was a slight decline between 1945 and 1953, but then income inequality remained virtually flat until 1981. Between 1981 and 1989, it rose fairly sharply, from 15.4 to 17.9 percent.

The comparison of trends in income inequality and wealth inequality during the 1980s is revealing, particularly since the former has received so much attention in both professional economic journals and the mass media. The evidence presented above indicates that the level of wealth concentration was at a postwar high in 1989. The time series on income inequality indicates exactly the same result for the concentration of household income. Moreover, the run-up in wealth

inequality that characterized the 1980s had a twentieth-century prece-
dent only during the 1920s. A similar finding can be reported for
income inequality.

It is hard to provide a direct comparison of the degree of increase
in inequality for the two series because of limitations on data avail-
ability. The Gini coefficient for wealth inequality shows an increase
from 0.80 in 1983 to 0.84 in 1989. On the basis of the *Current
Population Report* series, the coefficient for income inequality rose from
0.41 to 0.43 over the same period.[2] The share of wealth held by the
top 5 percent of wealth holders increased from 56 to 61 percent over
these years, whereas the share of total income received by the top 5
percent of income recipients moved upward from 17.1 to 18.9 percent.
The change in wealth inequality was more pronounced even if the
years in question are 1977 to 1989, which includes the entire period of
growing income inequality. Over this period, the Gini coefficient for
income inequality increased by only 0.03, and the income share of the
top 5 percent by only 2.1 percentage points.

It was reported above that the bottom two quintiles of wealth holders experienced an absolute decline in average net worth (in real terms)
between 1983 and 1989. Were trends in real income comparable?
According to the *Current Population Report* series, the mean income of
each of the bottom two quintiles increased in real terms over the period (by 11 percent and 10 percent, compared to 27 percent for the top
5 percent of the distribution). However, it is striking that the average
real incomes of both the bottom quintile and the second-lowest were
actually slightly less in 1989 than in 1973, even though overall mean
income for the entire population had grown over this period.[3] Thus,
poorer households have seen their net worth declining at the same time
as their incomes were stagnating.

It is apparent that the time patterns of wealth inequality and
income inequality have been similar but not identical across the century. Income inequality was generally stable during the postwar years
until 1981, while wealth inequality fell sharply during the 1970s. What
can explain this discrepancy? One variable that appears to figure sig-
nificantly in movements in wealth inequality is the ratio of stock prices
to housing prices. Stocks are an asset held primarily by the upper classes, whereas housing is the major asset of the middle classes. If stock
prices increase relative to house prices, the share of wealth held by the
top wealth groups will rise.[4]

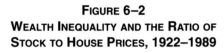

FIGURE 6–2
WEALTH INEQUALITY AND THE RATIO OF
STOCK TO HOUSE PRICES, 1922–1989

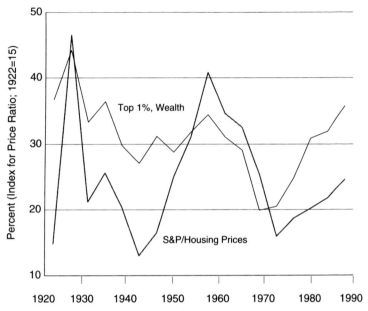

Source: Data from Appendix, Table A–1; U.S. Bureau of the Census, *Historical Statistics of the United States,* Part I (1975); U.S. Council of Economic Advisers (1992).

The ratio of stock prices to housing prices (indexed to a value of 15 in 1922 in order to fit the curve onto Figure 6–2) shows a time graph similar to that of wealth inequality. The ratio more than trebled between 1922 and 1929, corresponding to a tremendous growth in wealth inequality. It fell by half between the 1929 crash and 1933, as wealth inequality also declined, and then it increased by about 20 percent between 1933 and 1939 as the stock market partially recovered, which paralleled a new rise in wealth inequality. The price ratio then fell by almost half between 1939 and 1949 because of a rapid inflation in housing prices, which, in turn, was accompanied by a pronounced decline in wealth inequality.

The ratio of stock to housing prices more than trebled between 1949 and 1965, and this movement corresponded to a rise in wealth inequality. Between 1965 and 1979, the ratio fell by almost two-thirds, with most of the decline occurring after 1972. Before 1972 the main culprit was rising house prices, but subsequently the principal reason was a stagnating stock market. This period was not surprisingly characterized by a dramatic decline in wealth inequality. Between 1979 and 1989, the price ratio increased by more than half, as the stock market flourished, in line with the sharp increase in wealth inequality that was also recorded over this decade.[5]

➢ 7

CURRENT SYSTEMS OF WEALTH TAXATION

Given the high and rising degree of wealth inequality in the United States, it seems reasonable to consider the possibility of extending the tax base to include personal wealth holdings. Such a policy not only promotes greater equity in our society—particularly by targeting those who have a greater ability to pay—but may also provide households with an incentive for switching from less productive (those with a low rate of return) to more productive forms of assets. This chapter summarizes the forms of wealth taxation currently in place in the United States and other industrialized countries, as a preliminary to analyzing some of the potential effects of introducing direct wealth taxation.

THE UNITED STATES

Household wealth is currently taxed in two ways at the federal level in the United States: estate taxes and capital gains taxes. Federal estate taxes were first introduced in 1916, with major revisions in 1976 and 1981. Capital gains were included originally in the personal income tax system introduced into the country in 1913. Their provisions have been modified over time on a recurrent basis.[1]

ESTATE TAXES. The current system provides for the taxation of the value of an estate at the time of death of an individual. The tax is levied on the value of the estate, in contrast to the value of an inheritance received (see below for a discussion of the "inheritance tax"). Moreover, the estate tax system is integrated with the gift tax, which refers to the voluntary transfer of assets from one (living) individual to another. In principle, gifts are aggregated over the lifetime of the individual donor, and the lifetime aggregate of gifts is combined with the value of an estate at death. The estate tax applies to the full value of gifts and estates.[2]

As of 1992, each individual is exempted from estate taxes on net worth up to $600,000 (representing a unified tax credit of $192,800). Wealth above that amount is taxed at marginal rates that begin at 37 percent and reach as high as 55 percent (for estates over $2,500,000). For gifts, the first $10,000 per recipient ($20,000 in the case of a married couple) are exempt from the combined gift-estate tax. There is also full exemption for transfers (both gifts and estates) between spouses. All forms of wealth are included in the tax base for calculating the gift-estate tax except pension annuities and life insurance. Assets are appraised at market value at time of death, though special rules apply to farm property, closely held business, and unquoted stock and shares. Though there is no statutory provision for indexing tax thresholds to inflation, threshold changes over time have more than compensated for price rises. Several states also levy estate taxes, which are generally based on federal rules.

CAPITAL GAINS. Capital gains refer to the difference between the selling price and purchase price of an asset. There are some adjustments made for the value of capital improvements in the case of real property (such as a home). These are figured in on a cost basis when computing capital gains. In the United States, capital gains are taxed as part of the federal income tax system (and state income tax systems). Only realized capital gains are included (that is, capital gains on actual sales of assets).

As of 1992, capital gains were basically taxed at a 28 percent flat rate on both short-term and long-term gains.[3] However, in the case of owner-occupied housing, there is no tax levied on capital gains when a new primary residence is purchased whose price exceeds the selling price of the old home. In the case of individuals over the age of fifty-five, there is a one-time exclusion of $125,000 in capital gains. Tax liability on capital gains on gifts is deferred until the asset is sold. Capital gains on assets that enter an estate at time of death are exempt from taxation.

OTHER OECD COUNTRIES[4]

Other member countries of the OECD have much more exten-
sive taxation of household wealth. Besides taxation of estates at death
and of capital gains, many countries also impose direct taxation on
household wealth.

DIRECT WEALTH TAXATION. As of 1990, eleven OECD countries
had systems in place with direct taxation of household wealth: Austria,
Denmark, Finland, Germany, Luxembourg, the Netherlands, Norway,
Spain, Sweden, and Switzerland (see Table 7–1). In addition, France
had such a system in place from 1982 to 1987 and Ireland from 1975 to
1977.[5] Also, with the exception of Spain, most of these systems have
been in place for at least sixty years. In all eleven countries, the wealth
tax is administered in conjunction with the personal income tax. In
all cases except Germany, a joint tax return is filed for both income
and wealth. Though actual provisions vary among these countries, the
basic structure of the tax is very similar in each.

Countries differ in terms of the level at which the wealth tax takes
effect. The thresholds for married couples with two children range from
a low of $9,000 in Luxembourg to a high of $155,000 in Denmark. In
Germany, the threshold is $129,000; in the Netherlands, $51,000; and
in France, it was (when the tax was in effect) $520,000. These thresh-
old levels do not include the forms of wealth that are entirely excluded from the tax base (see below). Moreover, there are income exclusions
in many countries, so that a joint income-wealth threshold must be
passed in order for the wealth tax to become effective.

In several countries (such as Denmark, the Netherlands, and
Sweden), there are also ceilings on the total amount payable in income
and wealth taxes combined. These ceilings are usually expressed as a
percentage of taxable income (in the Netherlands, for example, it is
80 percent of taxable income).

Tax rates on household wealth tend to be low, on the order of a
few percent at most. Five countries have a flat-rate system: Austria (1.0
percent), Denmark (2.2 percent), Germany (0.5 percent), Luxembourg
(0.5 percent), and the Netherlands (0.8 percent). The other countries
have graduated marginal tax rates: Finland (1.5 percent at the threshold,
rising to 1.7 percent at $296,000), Norway (0.2 to 1.3 percent, the lat-
ter at $47,000), Spain (0.2 to 2.0 percent, the top rate at $7.1 million),

TABLE 7–1

WEALTH TAXATION SYSTEMS AMONG OECD COUNTRIES ON INDIVIDUAL OR FAMILY WEALTH HOLDINGS

	DIRECT WEALTH TAXATION	TRANSFER TAX AT DEATH AND ON GIFTS	CAPITAL GAINS TAXATION	WEALTH, DEATH, AND GIFT TAX RECEIPTS AS PERCENTAGE OF TOTAL TAX REVENUE[a]
Australia	No	None	Income	0.01
Austria	Yes	Inheritance	None	0.51
Belgium	No	Inheritance	None	0.58
Canada	No	None	Income	0.03
Denmark	Yes	Inheritance	Separate	0.92
Finland	Yes	Inheritance	Income	0.50
France	1982–87	Inheritance	Income	0.85
Germany	Yes	Inheritance	None	0.42
Greece	No	Inheritance	None	0.94
Iceland	Yes	Inheritance	Income	—
Ireland	1975–77	Inheritance	Separate	0.30
Italy	No	Estate/ Inheritance	None	0.23
Japan	No	Inheritance	Income	1.19
Luxembourg	Yes	Inheritance	Income	0.51
Netherlands	Yes	Inheritance	None	0.94
New Zealand	No	Estate	None	0.19
Norway	Yes	Inheritance	Income	0.61
Portugal	No	Inheritance	None	0.83
Spain	Yes	Inheritance	Income	0.49
Sweden	Yes	Inheritance	Income	0.68
Switzerland	Yes	Estate/ Inheritance	Income	3.06
Turkey	No	Inheritance	Income	0.19
United Kingdom	No	Estate	None	0.64
United States	No	Estate	Income	0.77

[a] Figures are for 1985.

Source: Organization for Economic Cooperation and Development (1988), p. 27.

Sweden (1.5 percent initially; reaching 3.0 percent at $140,000), and Switzerland (0.05 percent, rising to 0.30 percent at $334,000).[6]

Countries also vary in the forms of wealth that are included in the tax base. All the countries except Spain exempt household and personal effects. Most include the value of jewelry above a certain amount. All except Germany include the value of automobiles, and all include boats.

Several countries exempt savings accounts up to a certain level ($4,600 in Germany, for example). All exclude pension rights and pension-type annuities. Other forms of annuities are generally exempt. About half the countries exempt life insurance policies, while the other half include some portion of them in the tax base.

Owner-occupied housing is taxable in all eleven countries. However, in Austria and Finland a small deduction is allowed, while in the Netherlands and Norway housing is valued at only a small percentage of its actual market value. Other forms of wealth, including bonds, stocks and shares, and unincorporated businesses are included in the tax base in all countries.[7]

Most countries require an annual reassessment of the total value of personal property. However, Austria, Germany, and Luxembourg reassess every three years and Switzerland every two years. In principle, all eleven countries with a wealth tax system base the valuation of assets on current market value. However, in practice, this procedure is not always easy to enforce. First, some assets are not traded in the open market and hence do not have a readily available market price (small businesses and unquoted shares, for example). Second, housing presents a particular problem, since the usual method, based on the sale of "similar" property, depends in large measure on the definition of the similar class. On the other hand, bonds, quoted shares and stocks, and bank accounts are straightforward in their valuation.

Most countries use an "asset basis" to value unincorporated businesses, defined as the sum of the value of the individual assets contained in the business. This would typically understate the true value of the business, since no additional value is given to goodwill. Austria, Finland, and the Netherlands use a market value basis (the value of the business if it were sold immediately). Switzerland uses a formula based on the capitalized value of the business's profits over time.

Whereas most countries base their valuation of real property on its open market value, Austria uses a formula based on changes in the average costs of construction and changes in land prices. Germany uses the assessed valuation for local taxes. Luxembourg uses a formula based on the capitalized rental value of property.

DEATH TAXES. Twenty-two of the twenty-four OECD countries have death or gift taxes, or both (see Table 7–1). The only exceptions are Australia and Canada. However, most of the OECD countries have "inheritance taxes" in lieu of the American-style estate tax. The difference between the two is that inheritance taxes are assessed on the recipient, whereas an estate tax is assessed on the estate left by the decedent. With an inheritance tax, the tax schedule is applied to each individual bequest, whereas with an estate tax, the assessment is on the total value of the transfer. The inheritance tax has certain advantages over the estate tax. First, it can be adjusted more closely to the ability of an heir to pay. Second, preferential treatment can be accorded to immediate family, as opposed to more distant relatives or friends.[8]

Of the four countries with estate taxes—Italy, New Zealand, the United Kingdom, and the United States—the tax threshold varies from $20,000 for Italy to $600,000 for the United States. Marginal tax rates range from 3 to 31 percent in Italy, 30 to 60 percent in the United Kingdom, and 37 to 55 percent in the United States. In New Zealand, there is a flat rate of 40 percent. Spousal transfers are totally exempt in the United Kingdom and the United States but are taxed, with special treatment, in the other two countries. All four countries also have gift taxes. In Italy and the United States, these are aggregated over the person's lifetime and combined with the estate at death to determine the taxable base for the estate tax.

The structure of inheritance taxes is more complicated. Marginal tax rates vary with the relationship of the heir to the decedent, as do the tax thresholds. In France, for example, bequests to spouses have a threshold of $40,000, and the marginal tax rates vary from 5 to 40 percent, whereas bequests to nonrelatives have a threshold of $1,500 with a flat rate of 60 percent applied to the transfer. All nineteen OECD countries with an inheritance tax also have an associated gift tax.

CAPITAL GAINS TAXATION. Fifteen of the twenty-four OECD countries also provide for a tax on capital gains (see Table 7–1). All fifteen tax capital gains as they are realized (that is, at time of sale). In thirteen of the fifteen countries, capital gains are included as part of the personal income tax, whereas in the other two (Denmark and Ireland), a separate tax is collected. Interestingly, in eight countries—Denmark, Finland, Iceland, Luxembourg, Norway, Spain, Sweden, and Switzerland—there is both a direct wealth tax and a tax on capital gains.

There is wide latitude in the tax treatment of these gains across countries. In the United States, capital gains are treated similarly to ordinary income, with no difference between short-term and long-term gains (except in the case of capital losses). In Denmark, there is a flat rate of 50 percent; while in Switzerland, marginal rates range from 10 to 40 percent. In both these cases as well, there is no separate treatment of short-term gains.

In Australia, Norway (with some exceptions), and Spain, both short-term and long-term gains are treated as ordinary income and taxed in accordance with the personal income tax schedule. In Canada, three-quarters of capital gains are included as ordinary income. In Japan, half of long-term capital gains are taxed as ordinary income, while short-term gains are treated as ordinary income. In Sweden, a proportion of long-term gains are taxed as ordinary income, with the proportion depending on the nature of the property and the period held, while short-term gains are treated as ordinary income.

In most countries with capital gains taxes, gains on principal residences are exempt from taxation. Exceptions are Switzerland, where such gains are fully taxable; Japan, where the first $178,000 of gains are exempt; Spain, where exemption is subject to the purchase of a new residence; and Sweden and the United States, where only the excess of the sale price over the purchase price of a new residence is subject to taxation.

REVENUE COLLECTION. Though on the books these wealth taxation mechanisms appear to be a formidable way of collecting revenue, in fact, such levies account for only a very small part of total tax revenue in the various OECD countries. The last column of Table 7–1 summarizes the total tax collections from direct wealth and death/gift taxes as a percentage of total government revenue in 1985. Unfortunately, these totals do not include capital gains tax, since it is very hard to break out from regular income tax receipts. Among the twenty-three countries shown here, the average percentage is only 0.67. The shares range from a low of 0.01 percent in Australia to a high of 3.06 percent in Switzerland. Switzerland is, moreover, the only country in which the direct wealth tax collects more than 1 percent of total revenue—2.25 percent in 1985. The United States is slightly above average, with 0.77 percent of its total tax revenue from estate and gift taxes (of which 0.74 is from estate taxes and 0.03 from gift taxes). In terms of the receipts from death and gift taxes as a share of the total personal tax intake, the United States ranks fifth among OECD countries, after Japan, Greece, Portugal, and Switzerland. For 1991, total federal tax collections from estate and gift taxes in the United States amounted to $11.1 billion, or 1.1 percent of total tax revenues.[9]

One may wonder why these wealth taxes collect so little revenue, particularly when some of them have been in place for more than seventy years, plenty of time for refinement of their efficacy. Three possible reasons suggest themselves. First, particularly in Europe, tax proceeds from the personal income tax and the value-added tax on consumption are already quite substantial, so that relative to total tax revenues wealth tax collections appear small. This is particularly germane to countries such as Sweden that have a cap on combined income and wealth taxes. Second, there is the strong possibility of evasion or non-criminal avoidance. Unlike labor earnings and interest and dividend payments, which can be recorded at their source, it is much more difficult for a tax collection agency to obtain independent information on the financial securities, stock holdings, unquoted shares, or value of a family business owned by a household. Though real property must be registered with local tax authorities, there is still a possibility that its value will be underestimated for tax purposes.

A third and related reason is that it is easy to transfer financial wealth holdings across borders. With the exception of real property and most small businesses, a family normally can purchase assets outside the country of residence with ease. A country that imposes an excessive wealth tax may induce substantial capital flight. As a result, most countries with a wealth tax try to keep it more or less in line with that of other countries.

➢ 8

SIMULATIONS OF DIRECT WEALTH TAXATION IN THE UNITED STATES

This chapter provides simulation results of the potential revenue effects of three alternative wealth taxation systems as applied to U.S. household economic data. These are based on the actual tax codes of Germany, Sweden, and Switzerland. The distinctive characteristics of each plan are shown in Table 8–1.[1]

The simulations were performed on the basis of the 1989 U.S. personal income tax schedules and the 1989 *Survey of Consumer Finances*.[2] While the data are not perfect, the results are encouraging.[3] Even a very modest wealth tax (like the Swiss system, with marginal tax rates ranging from 0.05 percent to 0.30 percent and an exclusion of about $50,000 in wealth) could have raised $38 billion in 1989 or about $45 billion today. In light of the recent monumental efforts necessary to close the federal budget deficit by $50 billion, such a tax would go a long way toward achieving fiscal probity. Moreover, in the process only 3 percent of families would have seen their federal tax bill rise by more than 10 percent.

Simulations of alternative schemes for wealth taxation also suggest that a combined income-wealth taxation system may indeed be more equitable than our current income tax system. The wealth tax is, not surprisingly, progressive with respect to wealth. Its incidence would also fall more heavily on older households than younger ones (older

TABLE 8-1
DETAILS OF DIRECT WEALTH TAXATION SYSTEMS OF GERMANY, SWEDEN, AND SWITZERLAND

	GERMANY	SWEDEN	SWITZERLAND
A. *Thresholds*			
1. Single persons	$33,000	$56,000	$34,000
2. Married couple, no children	$57,000	$56,000	$56,000
3. Married couple, two children	$129,000	$56,000	$56,000
B. *Tax Rate Schedules*	Flat rate of 0.5 %	1.5% (to $28,000) 2.0% (next $28,000) 2.5% (next $140,000) 3.0% (over $196,000)	0.05% (to $83,000) 0.10% (next $139,000) 0.15% (next $225,000) 0.20% (next $333,000) 0.25% (next $333,000) 0.30% (over $1,113,000)
C. *Exclusions*	Household Effects Automobiles Savings (up to $4,600) Pensions/Annuities Life Insurance (up to $4,600) Unincorporated business (up to $58,000; excess taxed at 75%)	Household Effects Pensions/Annuities Life Insurance	Household Effects Pensions/Annuities
D. *Ceiling*	None	75 percent up to $50,000 of taxable income; 80 percent on excess.	None

Source: Organization for Economic Cooperation and Development (1988).

households tend to be wealthier), on married couples than singles (the former are also richer, on average), and on white individuals than non-whites (white families are generally much wealthier). Although this approach does not take into account behavioral responses of families to the imposition of a wealth tax, the calculations can nonetheless give some guidance as to the overall magnitude of likely revenues and redistributional effects.

There are three questions of interest. First, how much additional tax revenue will be raised under each alternative wealth taxation scheme (revenue effects)? Second, which groups will likely bear the burden of the new taxation of wealth (incidence effects)? Third, how will the alternative wealth tax systems affect overall inequality in the population and within different demographic groups (distributional effects)?

REVENUE EFFECTS

The actual U.S. personal income tax produces revenues of $445.7 billion, or 11.4 percent of total family income (details are tabulated in Table 8–2). A wealth tax following the German system would have produced total additional tax revenues of $67.5 billion in 1989, or 1.7 percent of total income. Adopting the German-style wealth tax would increase tax revenues by 15 percent overall. Imposing the Swedish wealth tax, in contrast, would have added an additional $328.7 billion of personal taxes, amounting to 8.4 percent of total income and increasing the total tax intake by 74 percent. The Swiss wealth tax would have raised $34.0 billion in taxes, representing 0.9 percent of total income and 8 percent of the total income tax proceeds. The Swedish wealth tax would thus have a massive effect on total tax revenues, while the other two would have moderate effects. However, even the German- and Swiss-style wealth taxes would yield new revenues considerably in excess of the actual collections from the estate and gift taxes, $8.7 billion in 1989.[4]

INCIDENCE

The incidence of wealth taxes depends on the joint distribution of income and wealth. If the two were perfectly correlated, then everyone would experience a similar proportional increase in taxes (depending on

TABLE 8–2

ORIGINAL INCOME TAX AND NEW WEALTH TAXES
AS PERCENTAGE OF FAMILY INCOME FOR ALTERNATIVE WEALTH TAXATION SYSTEMS
BY INCOME CLASS, WEALTH CLASS, AGE GROUP, FAMILY TYPE, AND RACE, 1989

	Original U.S. Income Tax	German Wealth Tax		Swedish Wealth Tax		Swiss Wealth Tax	
		Percentage of Income	Ratio to Income Tax	Percentage of Income	Ratio to Income Tax	Percentage of Income	Ratio to Income Tax
ALL FAMILIES	11.4	1.7	0.15	8.4	0.74	0.9	0.08
A. INCOME CLASS							
Under $5,000	0.0	1.3	—	0.0	—	0.6	—
$5,000-$9,999	1.1	0.9	0.76	0.7	0.57	0.3	0.27
$10,000-$14,999	3.1	1.1	0.35	2.3	0.75	0.5	0.15
$15,000-$24,999	5.2	1.4	0.27	4.2	0.82	0.7	0.13
$25,000-$49,999	8.0	1.1	0.13	5.0	0.62	0.5	0.06
$50,000-$74,999	11.2	0.9	0.08	5.0	0.45	0.4	0.04
$75,000-$99,999	13.5	1.7	0.13	8.8	0.66	0.8	0.06
$100,000 & over	17.1	3.0	0.18	15.7	0.92	1.7	0.10

B. WEALTH CLASS

Under $25,000	7.2	0.0	0.00	0.0	0.00	0.0	0.00
$25,000-$49,999	8.3	0.0	0.00	0.0	0.00	0.0	0.00
$50,000-$74,999	9.2	0.1	0.02	0.4	0.05	0.2	0.02
$75,000-$99,999	9.4	0.3	0.03	1.4	0.15	0.5	0.05
$100,000-$249,999	10.8	0.7	0.07	4.2	0.39	0.4	0.04
$250,000-$499,999	12.9	1.8	0.14	10.3	0.80	0.4	0.03
$500,000-$999,999	14.4	3.1	0.22	17.8	1.24	1.0	0.07
$1,000,000 & over	17.2	5.7	0.33	25.5	1.48	3.2	0.19

C. AGE GROUP

Under 35	9.2	0.5	0.05	2.3	0.25	0.3	0.03
35-54	12.3	1.2	0.09	6.6	0.54	0.6	0.05
55-69	11.9	3.2	0.27	14.6	1.22	1.5	0.13
70 and over	10.5	4.1	0.39	16.9	1.60	1.9	0.18

D. FAMILY TYPE

Married Couple	11.7	1.8	0.15	9.3	0.79	1.0	0.08
Males, Unmarried	12.3	1.5	0.12	5.9	0.48	0.7	0.05
Females, Unmarried	8.9	1.5	0.17	5.9	0.66	0.6	0.06

E. RACE

White	11.9	1.9	0.16	9.2	0.77	0.9	0.08
Nonwhite	8.7	0.9	0.10	3.9	0.44	0.5	0.05

Source: Author's own calculations from the *Survey of Consumer Finances* (1989). See text for details on tax calculations.

the wealth tax schedule). However, income and wealth are far from perfectly correlated. There are certain groups, such as the elderly, that have large wealth holdings but relatively little income. On the other hand, some young households may have high earnings but relatively little wealth accumulation (the "yuppies"). This new tax may thus shift the burden away from young households onto elderly ones.

Table 8–2 shows estimates of the new effective tax rates by income class, wealth class, age group, family type, and race.[5] The Swedish wealth tax system, like the graduated income tax in this country, is highly progressive with respect to income, rising from 0 percent for the lowest income class to 15.7 percent for the highest. Moreover, the proportionate increase in total taxes paid would be somewhat higher for upper-income families than lower-income ones. In contrast, both the German and Swiss wealth tax systems tend to lay claim to an almost constant percentage of income, except for the highest income class, which would pay a greater share with respect to its earnings. Moreover, in both cases, lower-income families would see their total tax bill rise proportionately more than higher-income families. While this may appear unfair, one must remember that the tax does not fall uniformly on lower-income families. Only a household with much wealth, regardless of income, would be liable for taxation. Any household with substantial net worth may legitimately be viewed as capable of contributing to the public good.

The American income tax system is also progressive with respect to household wealth, with tax rates on income rising from 7.2 percent for the lowest wealth class (under $25,000) to 17.2 percent for the richest ($1,000,000 or more). All three European wealth tax systems, not surprisingly, are also progressive with respect to wealth. Tax rates measured as a percentage of income would rise from zero for the lowest wealth class to 5.7 percent for the highest under the German tax system; from zero to 25.5 percent under the Swedish system; and from zero to 3.2 percent under the Swiss system. The proportionate increase in taxes would also be greater for wealthier families than poorer ones under all three systems.

Refer again to Table 8–2. Income tax rates show relatively little variation across age groups, rising from 9.2 percent for the youngest families to 12.3 percent for those 35–54, then falling back a bit for older cohorts. In contrast, under all three wealth tax systems, tax rates on income would rise monotonically with age group, reflecting the fact that wealth-income ratios increase with age. Under the German system, tax rates would range from 0.5 to 4.1 percent; under the Swedish system, from 2.3 to 16.9 percent; and under the Swiss system, from 0.3 to 1.9 percent. Under all three systems, taxes would increase proportionately more for older Americans than younger ones.

There is also relatively little variation in income tax rates by family type. Unmarried males face the highest average income tax rates, 12.3 percent, followed by married couples (11.7 percent) and single females (8.9 percent). Under all three wealth tax systems, married couples would face the highest tax rates, with unmarried male and female households taxed almost identically. Under the German system, married couples would pay 1.8 percent of income in wealth taxes, compared to 1.5 percent for unmarried males or females; in the Swedish system, the respective rates are 9.3 and 5.9 percent, and in the Swiss system, 1.0 and 0.7 percent.

White families generally pay higher tax rates than nonwhites— 11.9 percent compared to 8.7 percent—reflecting the higher relative incomes of whites. Under all three wealth tax systems, white families, on average far better endowed than minority families, would pay considerably higher taxes than nonwhites. Also, in all three cases, white families would see their tax bill rise proportionately more than nonwhite families.

DISTRIBUTIONAL EFFECTS

One can measure the effect of wealth taxation on inequality in three steps. First, figure out the inequality (based on the Gini coefficient) in the distribution of pretax income. Second, calculate the Gini coefficient of aftertax income resulting only from the imposition of the personal income tax. Third, compute the same measure for aftertax income resulting from both the income tax and each of the wealth tax systems. The distributional effect of the wealth tax will depend on its progressivity with respect to income, its magnitude, and the proportionate increase in taxes it generates by income class.

Results are shown in panel A of Table 8–3. Among all families, the Gini coefficient for pretax income is 0.52 in 1989. The Gini coefficient for income after income taxes is 0.50, indicating that the

Table 8–3

Distributional Effects of Alternative Wealth Taxation Systems
by Age Group, Family Type, and Race, 1989

| | | AGE GROUP | | | | FAMILY TYPE | | | RACE | |
	ALL	18-34	35-54	55-69	70+	MARRIED COUPLE	UNMARRIED MALE	UNMARRIED FEMALE	WHITE	NONWHITE
A. GINI COEFFICIENTS FOR INCOME										
Pretax Income	.521	.441	.477	.568	.568	.473	.529	.451	.504	.525
Original Posttax Income	.497	.420	.454	.543	.539	.446	.502	.426	.479	.503
New Post-Income/ German Wealth Tax	.495	.421	.451	.537	.534	.442	.501	.424	.477	.503
New Post-Income/ Swedish Wealth Tax	.476	.414	.434	.505	.487	.421	.487	.415	.458	.490
New Post-Income/ Swiss Wealth Tax	.495	.420	.452	.539	.536	.444	.502	.425	.477	.503

TABLE 8–3 (CONTINUED)

DISTRIBUTIONAL EFFECTS OF ALTERNATIVE WEALTH TAXATION SYSTEMS
BY AGE GROUP, FAMILY TYPE, AND RACE, 1989

| | AGE GROUP | | | | | FAMILY TYPE | | | RACE | |
	ALL	18-34	35-54	55-69	70+	MARRIED COUPLE	UNMARRIED MALE	UNMARRIED FEMALE	WHITE	NONWHITE
B. GINI COEFFICIENTS FOR INCOME* a										
Pretax Income*	.544	.453	.499	.599	.603	.500	.549	.468	.526	.542
Original Posttax Income*	.527	.435	.482	.583	.586	.481	.528	.449	.509	.524
New Post-Income*/ German Wealth Tax	.522	.433	.478	.577	.578	.475	.524	.445	.504	.521
New Post-Income*/ Swedish Wealth Tax	.502	.426	.460	.550	.548	.453	.509	.430	.483	.510
New Post-Income*/ Swiss Wealth Tax	.524	.434	.480	.580	.582	.478	.526	.447	.506	.522

a Income* is defined as family income plus 3.28 percent of family net worth.

Source: Author's own calculations from the *Survey of Consumer Finances* (1989). See text for details on tax calculations.

personal income tax system has a modest equalizing effect on income distribution. Adding the Swedish wealth tax to the personal taxation formula results in a further reduction of the Gini coefficient to 0.48. The Swedish wealth tax thus has an equalizing effect on the income distribution similar in magnitude to the personal income tax system. However, neither the German nor the Swiss wealth tax has much effect on measured income inequality, mainly because of the small amount of revenue that they generate and their lack of progressivity with respect to income.

The distributional effect of the wealth tax systems does show some variation by age group, family type, and race. The equalizing effects of the wealth tax exert greater influence within older age groups than among younger ones. For age group seventy and over, the imposition of the Swedish wealth tax system causes the Gini coefficient to fall from 0.54 to 0.49. The effects are stronger among married couples than unmarried individuals: among married couples, the Gini coefficient declines from 0.45 to 0.42 when Swedish wealth taxes are added to income taxes. The equalizing effect is also larger among white families than among nonwhite ones.

Panel B of Table 8–3 shows the same set of computations for an alternate measure of income called Income*. Income* is defined as family income plus 3.28 percent of family net worth (3.28 percent is an estimate of the average annual real rate of appreciation on household wealth over the 1962–89 period). Income* is logically a more inclusive measure of family welfare than normal income. The effects of a wealth tax on this more inclusive measure of income may be considered a better measure of the overall distributional effects of a wealth tax.

Results for Income* are quite similar to those for standard family income. Among all families, the Gini coefficient is 0.544 for pretax Income*, 0.527 for Income* after the payment of income taxes, and 0.502 for Income* after both income and Swedish wealth taxes are paid. As before, the German and Swiss wealth tax systems have little distributional impact. The equalizing effects of wealth taxes on the distribution of Income* increase with age, are greater for married couples than for singles, and are stronger among white than nonwhite families.

➤ 9

CONCLUDING REMARKS

The pronounced rise in wealth inequality during the 1980s creates some urgency in policy remedies. The most telling statistic is that *virtually all* the growth in (marketable) wealth between 1983 and 1989 accrued to the top 20 percent of households. Indeed, the bottom 40 percent of households saw their wealth decline in absolute terms. This was compounded by the stark reality of a growing proportion of households with zero or negative net worth. The results are even more extreme for financial wealth.

What, if anything, should be done about this? If one policy goal is to moderate the rising inequality of recent years, direct taxation of wealth is one proposed remedy.[1] This would compensate for the reduced progressivity of the income tax system. The 1980s witnessed falling marginal tax rates on income, particularly for the rich and very rich. Though the 1993 budget bill passed by Congress and signed into law by President Clinton will raise the marginal income tax rates on the very rich, they will still be considerably lower than at the beginning of the 1980s (and much lower than in the 1960s).

Currently, wealth is taxed in only two forms on the federal level: estate taxes (at death) and capital gains taxes (on realized capital gains). Eleven OECD countries currently have direct taxation on wealth (three others have had such a system in the past), and most of these are in conjunction with a death tax and a capital gains tax.

What do the simulation results of the last chapter suggest? First, the current personal income tax system of this country helps mitigate the

51

disparities in earnings, but its overall effects are modest (indeed, they would probably appear even smaller if full information were available on itemized deductions and income adjustments). Second, of the three wealth tax systems considered, only the Swedish system has any noticeable equalizing effect, and even in this case the result is similarly modest. This is true even though the Swedish wealth tax would increase total tax revenues (over and above the personal income tax) by 74 percent. The German and Swiss systems would increase tax revenues by 15 and 8 percent, respectively—too small to have much distributional impact.

Third, these three wealth taxes have some desirable features from a demographic standpoint. All three tend to fall proportionately more on older families than younger ones; more on married couples than singles; and more on whites than nonwhites (whites are much wealthier than nonwhites). Moreover, the equalizing effects of the wealth taxes are greater among older families, married couples, and whites.

Fourth, even the very modest, Swiss-style system would have yielded an additional $38 billion of revenue in 1989, or about $45 billion today. In light of the demands on the federal budget, such a tax could be valuable indeed. In spite of the proposed tax's potency as a revenue-raising tool, only 3 percent of families would see their federal tax bill rise by more than 10 percent. In conclusion, a direct wealth taxation system—even one like Switzerland's—could ease the country's budgetary strains and provide greater equity across generational, racial, and familial categories. These characteristics argue in favor of its adoption in the United States.

OTHER RATIONALES FOR WEALTH TAXATION? Besides its desirable effects with regard to equity and revenue, are there any other characteristics of wealth taxation that may argue in its favor? Two other arguments have been advanced in support of a wealth tax. First, beyond considerations of overall ("vertical") equity, some have argued that a wealth tax can be justified in terms of "taxable capacity." Income alone is not a sufficient gauge of well-being or of the ability to pay taxes. The possession of wealth, over and above the income it yields directly, must be figured into the calculation. Two families with identical incomes but different levels of wealth are not equivalent in terms of their well-being, since a wealthier family will have more independence, firmer security in times of economic stress (such as occasioned by unemployment, illness, or family breakup), and readier access to consumer credit. Greater wealth thus confers on the affluent family a larger capacity to pay taxes; in the interests of "horizontal equity," wealth should be taxed directly as well as income.

A second argument is that an annual wealth tax may induce individuals to transfer their assets from less productive uses to more productive ones. A tax on wealth may provide an incentive to switch from low-yielding investments to high-yielding ones, in order to offset the additional taxes. For example, a wealth tax based on the market value of property might induce neglectful owners to seek to realize potential returns through development, renovation, or sale. Likewise, a wealth tax might induce individuals to seek more income-generating assets in place of conspicuous consumer durables such as luxury cars and yachts. A direct wealth tax has the added feature that it may inhibit the avoidance of income taxes by encouraging investors to switch assets into income-yielding forms.

It should be noted, too, that existing wealth taxation in this country works poorly. The estate tax has historically been an extremely porous tax (some refer to it as a "voluntary" tax). The thresholds have been raised over time (from $50,000 in 1916, when the estate tax was first instituted, to $60,000 in 1942, then to $175,000 in 1981, and to $600,000 in 1987),[2] so that only a very small percentage of estates (typically on the order of 1 percent) have been subject to estate tax. Estate taxes on assets can be avoided altogether by setting up a trust fund with children or other desired "heirs" as beneficiaries (though provisions for such trusts were tightened up in the 1993 federal tax legislation). Moreover, gift exclusions allow a considerable amount of wealth to be passed on before death exempt from taxation. In addition, there are the usual problems of underreporting, valuation of assets, and compliance (how to value a family business?).

Finally, the estate tax system has a provision that capital gains on assets are essentially excluded from consideration. Normally, realized capital gains are counted as part of the taxable base in computing income taxes. However, if an asset is not sold and winds up in an estate, the capital gains are forgiven by the tax authorities. This loophole by itself probably more than equals the total revenue collected by the estate tax system. Given the history of estate taxes in this country and the vested interest of the wealthy in maintaining the current system (not to speak of the estate planners and lawyers who profit from the system), it may be easier politically to institute a new wealth tax than to try to revamp the existing estate tax regime.

Counterarguments

Perhaps the strongest argument against direct wealth taxation is that it will inhibit savings and lower capital investment. One unavoidable implication of wealth taxation is that the (after-tax) return to capital will be lowered. By exerting a strong disincentive on the already low U.S. savings rate, it may simply encourage increased consumption. Another possibility is that a wealth tax, by lowering the after-tax rate of return on financial assets, may encourage families to invest in non-financial assets, such as certain forms of real estate, collectibles, precious metals, luxury items, and the like. The search for greater opacity to thwart the Internal Revenue Service could perversely result in shifting of household portfolios to unproductive uses; though, as suggested above, one can reasonably argue the opposite case—that taxing both income-yielding and non-income-yielding forms of wealth will induce households to shift to higher-yielding assets.

One simple, though relatively crude, way of addressing this issue is to compare the average savings rates of countries with direct wealth taxes to those without such taxes. On the basis of OECD national accounts data, within both sets of countries there is large variation in average household savings rates over the period 1980–90.[3] Among those with a wealth tax, savings rates range from 4.0 percent for Spain to 8.2 percent for Germany, 9.1 percent for the Netherlands, and 10.5 percent for Switzerland. Among those without a wealth tax, figures range from 3.6 percent for the United Kingdom to 5.7 percent for the United States and 11.6 percent for Japan. The average savings rates among countries with a wealth tax is 8.0 percent, and that for countries without a wealth tax is 9.8 percent. It is far from clear that taxation of wealth explains these differences. Is the high savings rate in Japan due to low taxation of wealth? On the surface, at least, there appears to be no strong evidence that the presence of a wealth tax inhibits savings.

A second potential problem stemming from a wealth tax is capital flight. By inserting a wedge between what an asset earns and what the owner receives, a tax understates the return in the owner's eyes and encourages the owner to look for higher returns elsewhere. This argument applies to every tax, however, and if capital indeed moved like quicksilver, it would render any taxation of capital and wealth all but impossible. The very fact that the wealth tax proposal presented below is based on the Swiss model suggests that capital flight is unlikely to be a serious concern. Like Switzerland, the United States is a safe haven for international wealth, a status unlikely to be threatened by the very low tax rates suggested here.

A WEALTH TAX FOR THE UNITED STATES

The time now is ripe for the introduction of a personal tax on wealth holdings. The statistics point to an enormous degree of inequality in household net worth in this country today, and an even greater degree in terms of household financial wealth. On the grounds of (horizontal) equity, a combination of annual income and the current stock of wealth provides a better gauge of the ability to pay taxes than income alone. Moreover, there is no evidence from other advanced economies that the imposition of a modest direct tax on household wealth has had a deleterious effect on personal savings or overall economic growth. In fact, there are arguments to the contrary, that such a tax may induce a more efficient allocation of household wealth, toward more productive uses. Finally, the possibility that such a levy might promote capital flight is not borne out by the evidence.

Most appropriate for the United States would be a wealth tax modeled after the Swiss system. The basic exclusion could begin at $100,000. The marginal tax structure might look as follows: 0.05 percent (applied to household wealth valued from $100,000 to $199,999); 0.10 percent (from $200,000 to $349,999); 0.15 percent (from $350,000 to $499,999); 0.20 percent (from $500,000 to $749,999); 0.25 percent (from $750,000 to $999,999); and 0.30 percent ($1,000,000 and above). As in the Swiss system, all household effects, pensions, and annuities would be excluded.[4] In addition, the rules would provide a $10,000 exemption on automobiles (that is, only expensive cars would be subject to the tax).

The wealth tax would be fully integrated with the personal income tax. The same tax form could be used for both. The family would be required to list the value of all assets and debts on a new subsidiary form (say, "Schedule W"). Verification of most of the assets and debts would be administratively easy to implement. Insofar as banks and other financial institutions provide records to the Internal Revenue Service (IRS) that list interest payments, such documents could be modified to include also the value of the interest-bearing accounts as of a certain date (say, December 31). A similar procedure could be applied to dividend forms.

Moreover, financial institutions that provide the Internal Revenue Service with information on mortgage payments made by households could now add the value of the outstanding mortgage. Other types of loans (and loan payments) could be similarly recorded by these institutions. Insurance companies could provide the IRS with statements on the value of life insurance equity (they already send these to individuals).

The two main stumbling blocks are the current market value of owner-occupied housing (and other real estate) and the valuation of unincorporated businesses. For the former, there are several possible solutions, some of which are currently in use in other countries. The family could be asked to estimate the current market value (as is now done in household surveys). Alternatively, it could be asked to list the original purchase price and date of purchase, and the IRS could use a regional (or locale-specific) price index based on housing survey data to update the value. Another method would ask residents to provide the figure for assessed valuation of the property, and the IRS could provide a locale-specific adjustment factor, based on periodic survey data, to estimate current market value.

For unincorporated businesses, the simplest technique is to accumulate the value of individual assets invested in the business over time (these figures are already provided in Form C of the personal tax return). Another possibility is to capitalize the net profit figures (also provided on Form C), as the Swiss currently do.

Calculations show that such a tax structure would yield an average tax rate on household wealth (as of 1989) of 0.2 percent. Previous work indicates that the *real* rate of return on household wealth over the period from 1962 to 1989 averaged 3.28 percent per year.[5] Thus, the new tax regime would reduce the average yield on household assets by only 6 percent. Even the top marginal tax rate of 0.3 percent would reduce the average yield on personal wealth by only 9 percent. These figures suggest that disincentive effects, if any, on personal savings would be very modest.

Would such a tax be popular? Of course, no additional payment of taxes is likely to be cheered by the American people. But the proposed wealth tax would affect a very small percentage of the population. Only 3 percent of American families would see their overall personal tax bill (combining income and wealth taxes) rise by more than 10 percent. A full 78 percent would see their tax bill rise by no more than 1 percent, if at all. (In fact, two-thirds of households would fall below the $100,000 threshold and would therefore be exempted from paying.)

About 40 billion dollars would be raised from levying such a tax in 1994 (somewhat less than would be raised by an exact copy of the Swiss system). This is not a large amount, representing about 3 percent of total federal tax receipts. However, on the margin such additional revenue could be critical. Even at this writing, there is discussion in the U.S. Congress of efforts to implement a major overhaul of the U.S. welfare system. The main stumbling block, as reported on the front page of the *New York Times*, is the need to raise an additional 15 billion dollars over five years. In this political environment, an extra 40 billion dollars *per year* could provide the fiscal latitude to enact important legislative initiatives. A direct annual tax on personal wealth could thus be a valuable addition to the fiscal toolbox available to the federal government.

POSTSCRIPT

With the release of the 1992 Survey of Consumer Finances (SCR) in April of 1996, it is now possible to update some of the earlier figures to 1992. The results of Chapter 3, based on the 1983 and 1989 Surveys of Consumer Finances, presented evidence of sharply increasing household wealth inequality over this period. The addendum examines whether this trend continued over the period 1989–1992. It also presents later figures on racial disparities in household wealth, as well as more recent changes in the composition of wealth.[1]

THE COMPOSITION OF HOUSEHOLD WEALTH

As in earlier years, owner-occupied housing was the most important household asset in 1992, accounting for 29 percent of total assets. However, net home equity (the value of the house minus any outstanding mortgage) amounted to less than 20 percent of total assets. Real estate, other than owner-occupied housing, comprised 15 percent, and business equity 20 percent of total assets.

COMPOSITION OF TOTAL HOUSEHOLD WEALTH
1983, 1989, AND 1992[a]
(PERCENT OF GROSS ASSETS)

	1983	1989	1992
Owner-occupied housing (gross value)	30.1	28.5	28.7
Other real estate (gross value)	14.9	13.2	14.9
Business equity	18.8	16.2	20.0
Total deposits[b]	15.3	12.4	10.0
Life insurance (cash surrender value)	1.5	1.6	1.7
Pension accounts[c]	2.2	3.0	7.0
Financial securities	4.2	5.8	4.9
Corporate stock and mutual funds	9.0	11.6	7.8
Net equity in personal trusts	2.6	3.1	2.6
Other assets[d]	1.3	4.5	2.4
Total	100.0	100.0	100.0
Total debt[e]	13.1	14.1	15.1
Addendum			
Net home equity[f]	23.8	20.3	19.3
Debt/equity ratio	0.151	0.165	0.178

a. Source: own computations from the 1983, 1989, and 1992 Surveys of Consumer Finances.

b. Checking accounts, savings accounts, time deposits, money market funds and certificates of deposits.

c. IRAs, Keogh plans, 401(k) plans, the accumulated value of defined contribution pension plans, and other retirement accounts.

d. Gold and other precious metals, royalties, jewelry, antiques, furs, loans to friends and relatives, future contracts, and miscellaneous assets.

e. Mortgage, installment, consumer, and other debt.

f. Gross value of owner-occupied housing less home mortgage debt.

Demand deposits, time deposits, money market funds, and CDs made up 10 percent, pension accounts 7 percent, and the cash surrender value of life insurance less than 2 percent. Bonds and other financial securities amounted to 6 percent; corporate stock, including mutual funds, to 8 percent; and trust equity to a little over 3 percent. Debt as a proportion of gross assets was 15 percent, and the debt-equity ratio (the ratio of total household debt to net worth) was 0.18.

There have been some important changes in the composition of household wealth during the period between 1983 and 1992. The most notable is that pension accounts rose from 2.2 to 7.0 percent of total assets. This increase almost exactly offset the decline in total deposits, from 15.3 to 10.0 percent of assets, so that it is reasonable to conclude that households have substituted tax-free pension accounts for taxable savings deposits.

Gross housing wealth fell from 30.1 to 28.5 percent of total assets between 1983 and 1989, but then increased slightly to 28.7 percent in 1992. Moreover, according to the SCF data, the homeownership rate (the percent of families owning their own home, including mobile homes), after falling from 63.4 percent in 1983 to 62.8 percent in 1989, picked up to 64.1 percent in 1992.

In contrast, net equity in owner-occupied housing has fallen continuously, from 23.8 percent at the beginning of the period to 19.3 percent at the end. The difference between the two series is attributable to the changing magnitude of mortgage debt on homeowner's property, which increased from 21 percent in 1983 to 29 percent in 1989 and 33 percent in 1992. In fact, overall indebtedness increased over the period. The ratio of total debt to total assets creeped up from 13.1 percent in 1983 to 14.1 percent in 1989 and to 15.1 percent in 1992. The debt-equity ratio rose from 15.1 percent in 1983 to 17.8 percent in 1992. Moreover, the fraction of household recording zero or negative net worth jumped from 15.5 percent in 1983 to 17.9 percent in 1989 and to 18.3 percent in 1992.

The proportion of total assets in the form of other (non-home) real estate was the same in 1992 as in 1983. Business equity increased somewhat as a share of gross wealth between 1983 and 1992, from 18.8 to 20.0 percent, while the value of stocks and mutual funds fell slightly, from 9.0 to 7.8 percent of assets. However, the total value of business equity and corporate stocks was almost identical in

1983, 1989, and 1992. Financial securities increased slightly in
importance in the household portfolio, from 4.2 percent in 1983 to
4.9 percent in 1992, while the share of trust equity in total assets
also was identical in 1983 and 1992.

This tabulation provides a picture of the average holdings of all
families in the economy. But there are marked class differences in
how middle-class families and the rich invest their wealth. The richest 1 percent of households (as ranked by wealth) invested over 80
percent of their savings in investment real estate, businesses, corporate stock, and financial securities in 1992. Housing accounted for
only 8 percent of their wealth, and liquid assets another 11 percent.
Their ratio of debt to assets was 6 percent. Among the next richest
19 percent of U.S. households, housing comprised 30 percent of
their total assets and liquid assets another 25 percent. Forty-five percent of their assets took the form of investment assets—real estate,
business equity, stocks, and bonds. Debt amounted to 13 percent of
their total value of assets.

THE COMPOSITION OF HOUSEHOLD WEALTH
BY WEALTH CLASS IN 1992[a]
(PERCENT OF GROSS ASSETS)

	All Households	Top One%	Next 19%	Bottom 80%
Owner-occupied housing	28.7	8.0	30.3	62.8
Liquid assets (bank deposits, money market funds, cash surrender value of insurance and pension accounts)	18.7	11.0	25.0	21.2
Investment real estate and unincorporated businesses	34.9	52.4	28.0	10.1
Corporate stock, financial securities, personal trusts, and other assets	17.7	28.7	16.7	5.9
Total	100.0	100.0	100.0	100.0
Total debt	15.1	6.4	12.6	35.4

a. Source: own computations from the 1992 Survey of Consumer Finances. Households are classified into wealth class according to their net worth. Cut-off points are: top 1 percent, net worth of $2,420,000 or more; next 19 percent, net worth between $180,700 and $2,420,000; and bottom 80 percent, net worth less than $180,700.

In contrast, almost two-thirds of the wealth of the bottom 80 percent of households was invested in their own home. Another 21 percent went into monetary savings of one form or another. Together housing and liquid assets accounted for 84 percent of their total assets. Of the remaining 16 percent, about three-fifths was invested in non-home real estate and business equity and the other two-fifths in various financial assets and corporate stock. The ratio of debt to assets was 35 percent, much higher than for the richest 20 percent.

Another way to portray differences between middle class households and the rich is to compute the share of total assets of different types held by each group. In 1992 the richest 1 percent of households held half of all outstanding stock and trust equity, over half of financial securities and business equity, and 46 percent of investment real estate. The top 10 percent of families as a group accounted for about 90 percent of stock shares, bonds, trusts, and business equity, and over 80 percent of non-home real estate.

In contrast, owner-occupied housing, deposits, life insurance, and pension accounts were more evenly distributed among households. The bottom 90 percent of households accounted for almost two-thirds of the value of owner-occupied housing, over 40 percent of deposits, over half of life insurance cash value, and almost 40 percent of the value of pension accounts. Debt was the most evenly distributed component of household wealth, with the bottom 90 percent of households responsible for 63 percent of total indebtedness.

There was very little change between 1989 and 1992 in the concentration of asset ownership, with the notable exception of pensions. The share of total pension accounts held by the richest 10 percent of households increased from 53 to 62 percent over this period. The share of total debt owed by the top 10 percent also increased, from 30 to 38 percent.

THE PERCENT OF TOTAL ASSETS HELD BY WEALTH CLASS, 1992[a]

Asset Type	Share of Top 10%			Total	1989	1992
	Top 1.0%	Next 9%	Bottom 90%			

A. Assets Held Primarily by the Wealthy

Stocks	49.6	36.7	13.6	100.0	89.4	86.4
Bonds	62.4	28.9	8.7	100.0	88.7	91.3
Trusts	52.9	35.1	12.0	100.0	89.1	88.0
Business Equity	61.6	29.5	8.9	100.0	90.1	91.1
Non-Home Real Estate	45.9	37.1	17.0	100.0	80.1	83.0
Total for Group	54.4	33.3	12.3	100.0	87.1	87.7

B. Assets and Liabilities Held Primarily by the Non-Wealthy

Principal Residence	9.0	27.1	63.9	100.0	33.8	36.1
Deposits[b]	22.4	37.3	40.3	100.0	60.4	59.7
Life Insurance	10.0	35.1	54.9	100.0	44.7	45.1
Pension Accountsc	16.4	45.9	37.7	100.0	52.9	62.3
Total for Group	12.9	32.3	54.8	100.0	42.7	45.2

Total Debt	13.8	23.8	62.5	100.0	30.1	37.5

a. Source: own computations from the 1989 and 1992 Survey of Consumer Finances. Households are classified into wealth class on the basis of their net worth. The cut-off points for 1992 are as follows: Top 1 percent, net worth of $2,420,000 or more; next 9 percent, net worth between $355,250 and $2,420,000; bottom 90 percent, net worth less than $355,250.

b. Includes demand deposits, savings deposits, time deposits, money market funds, and certificates of deposit.

c. IRAs, Keogh plans, 401(k) plans, the accumulated value of defined contribution pension plans, and other retirement accounts.

CHANGES IN AVERAGE WEALTH

Median wealth increased by 8 percent between 1983 and 1989, from $47,000 to $50,800 (all figures are in 1992 dollars) and then declined sharply from $50,800 in 1989 to $42,900 in 1992, or by 15 percent. These results indicate that the average American household enjoyed some gains in their net worth during the 1980s but suffered a fairly precipitous drop in their wealth during the early 1990s. Mean wealth grew by 23 percent, from $183,000 in 1983 to $224,000 in 1989 but then fell off slightly from 1989 to 1992, by 5 percent. Median wealth thus declined considerably more between 1989 and 1992 than mean wealth holdings.

MEAN AND MEDIAN WEALTH AND INCOME, 1983, 1989, AND 1992[a]
(1992 DOLLARS)

	1983	1989	1992	% Change 1989–1992
Net Worth				
1. Median	46,998	50,846	43,235	-15.0
2. Mean	182,989	224,804	213,329	-5.1
Financial Wealth				
1. Median	10,151	11,773	10,250	-12.9
2. Mean	132,793	171,754	164,766	-4.1
Income				
1. Median	28,521	30,590	29,120	-4.8
2. Mean	38,340	44,970	43,535	-3.2

a. Sources: own computations from the 1983, 1989, and 1992 Survey of Consumer Finances.

Median financial wealth was a bare $10,000 in 1992. The average American household thus had very little savings available for their immediate needs. The time pattern for financial wealth is very similar to that for household net worth. Median financial wealth rose by 16 percent between 1983 and 1989 and then fell by 13 percent from 1989 to 1992. Mean financial wealth, after increasing by 29 percent from 1983 to 1989 declined slightly, by 4 percent, between 1989 and 1992.

Median household income, after growing sluggishly between 1983 and 1989, then declined by 5 percent between 1989 and 1992, from $30,600 to $29,100. Mean income grew by 17 percent from 1983 to 1989 but then declined by a modest 3 percent in the ensuing three years.

In sum, average household net worth, financial wealth, and income all fell between 1989 and 1992. However, the decline in median wealth was substantially greater than the decline in mean wealth.

RECENT TRENDS IN WEALTH INEQUALITY

The level of wealth inequality has fallen somewhat between 1989 and 1992. The share of wealth held by the top 1 percent fell by 1.8 percentage points, from 39.0 to 37.2 percent. Most of the loss was made up by the next 19 percentiles, so that the share of the top 20 percent fell only slightly, from 84.6 to 83.8 percent. The Gini coefficient also declined somewhat, from 0.840 in 1989 to 0.823 in 1992. However, wealth inequality in 1992 remained above its level in 1983. The share of the top 1 percent was 37.2 percent in 1992 and 33.8 percent in 1983, a difference of 3.4 percentage points; and the share of the top 20 percent was 2.5 percentage points greater in 1992. The Gini coefficient was 0.799 in 1983, compared to 0.823 in 1992.

Inequality of financial wealth showed a somewhat stronger decline between 1989 and 1992. The share of the top 1 percent fell by 2.7 percentage points, from 48.3 to 45.6 perce nt, and the share of the top 20 percent was down from 93.9 to 92.3 percent. The Gini coefficient fell from 0.929 to 0.903. As with net worth, financial wealth was still more unequally distributed in 1992 than in 1983.

Income inequality, as noted in Section 3, increased sharply between 1983 and 1989. However, there was very little change between 1989 and 1992. The share of the top 1 percent fell slightly, from 16.4 to 15.7 percent of total income, a decline that was offset by and increase in the share of the next 19 percent of households of 1.7 percentage points, while the Gini coefficient rose slightly, from 0.521 to 0.528.

PERCENTAGE SHARE OF TOTAL WEALTH AND INCOME HELD
BY PERCENTILE GROUP, 1983, 1989, AND 1992[a]

	Percentile Shares			
Year	Top 1.0%	Next 19%	Bottom 80%	Gini Coefficient
A. *Net Worth*				
1983	33.8	47.6	18.7	0.799
1989	39.0	45.6	15.4	0.840
1992	37.2	46.6	16.3	0.823
B. *Financial Wealth*				
1983	42.9	48.4	8.7	0.893
1989	48.3	45.8	6.1	0.929
1992	45.6	46.7	7.8	0.903
C. *Income*				
1983	12.8	39.0	48.1	0.480
1989	16.4	39.0	44.5	0.521
1992	15.7	40.7	43.7	0.528

a. Source: own computations from the 1983, 1989, and 1992 Surveys of Consumer Finances.

GAINS FROM THE ECONOMIC GROWTH OF THE *1980s*. Between 1989 and 1992 the biggest loss was sustained by the richest 1 percent, whose average wealth fell by $847,000 (in 1992 dollars) or almost 10 percent. The next 19 percent (ranked in terms of wealth) also sufferred a decline on their wealth, by 3 percent, whereas the mean wealth of the bottom 80 percent remained unchanged. Still, over the period from 1983 to 1992, the largest gains in relative terms were made by the wealthiest households. The top 1 percent saw their average wealth (in 1992 dollars) rise by 1.7 million dollars or by 28 percent and the next 19 percent by 14 percent; while the bottom 80 percent saw their wealth grow by a paltry 1 percent.

**MEAN WEALTH AND INCOME BY PERCENTILE GROUP, 1983, 1989,
AND 1992[a] (IN THOUSANDS, 1992 DOLLARS)**

Year	Top 1.0%	Next 19%	Bottom 80%	All
A. *Net Worth*				
1983	6,176	458.2	42.7	183.0
1989	8,772	539.2	43.3	224.8
1992	7,925	523.6	43.3	213.3
Percent Change in Mean Net Worth				
1983-89	42.0	17.7	1.4	22.9
1989-92	-9.7	-2.9	-0.1	-5.1
1983-92	28.3	14.3	1.3	16.6
Percent of Total Increase in Net Worth Accruing to Each Group				
1983-92	57.7	40.9	1.4	100.0
B. *Financial Wealth*				
1983	5,695	338.2	14.5	132.8
1989	8,292	412.7	13.0	171.8
1992	7,513	404.5	16.0	164.8
Percent Change in Mean Financial Wealth				
1983-89	45.6	22.0	-10.0	29.3
1989-92	-9.4	-2.0	22.5	-4.1
1983-92	31.9	19.6	10.3	24.1
Percent of Total Increase in Financial Wealth Accruing to Each Group				
1983-92	56.9	39.4	3.7	100.0
C. *Income*				
1983	518.8	83.0	24.3	38.3
1989	733.7	90.8	24.6	45.0
1992	671.8	91.7	23.3	43.5

Percent Change in Mean Household Income

1983-89	41.4	19.3	1.0	17.3
1989-92	-8.4	1.0	-5.0	3.2
1983-92	29.5	20.4	-4.1	13.6

Percent of Total Increase in Household Income Accruing to Each Group

1983-92	64.1	69.0	-33.0	100.0

a. Source: own computations from the 1983, 1989, and 1992 Surveys of Consumer Finances.

If we calculate the relative share of the total gain in wealth which accrues to different percentile groups, as we did in Section 3, the results are even starker. The top 20 percent of wealth holders received 99 percent of the total gain in wealth over the period from 1983 to 1992.[2] The top 1 percent alone enjoyed 58 percent of wealth growth. The bottom three quintiles actually saw their collective wealth fall by 150 billion dollars in 1992 dollars.

The pattern of results are quite similar for financial wealth. Between 1983 and 1992, 96 percent of the gains in the overall growth of financial wealth accrued to the top 20 percent and 57 percent to the top 1 percent.

A similar calculation using income data reveals that the only group to enjoy positive gains in real income over the period from 1983 to 1992 were households in the top 20 percent of the income distribution. Gains were greatest for the top 1 percent of households, whose mean income grew by 30 percent in real terms. The next 19 percent (ranked in terms of income) saw their average incomes increase by 20 percent, while the income of the bottom 80 percent fell by 4 percent. As a result, between 1983 and 1992, 133 percent of the growth of income accrued to the top 20 percent of income recipients and almost two thirds to the top 1 percent.

These results indicate rather dramatically that the growth in the economy during the period from 1983 to 1992 was concentrated in a surprisingly small part of the population, as was true for the period 1983 to 1989. The top quintile accounted for almost all of the wealth gain and more than 100 percent of the growth of income.

RACIAL DIFFERENCES

As discussed in Section 4, striking differences are also found in the wealth holdings of white and nonwhite households. For this purpose, households are divided into two groups: (1) non-Hispanic whites and (2) Hispanics, blacks, American Indians, and Asians. The average income of nonwhite and Hispanic households relative to the income of non-Hispanic white households remained almost constant between 1983 and 1992, at about 58 percent. The ratio of median income increased somewhat, from 61 to 64 percent over this period.[3]

In contrast, nonwhite and Hispanic households made substantial gains on non-Hispanic whites in terms of both mean and median wealth from 1983 to 1992. The ratio of mean wealth climbed steadily, from 0.24 to 0.33, while the ratio of median wealth, after slipping between 1983 and 1989, more than doubled between 1983 and 1992, from 0.09 to 0.20. Indeed, while both the mean and median wealth of non-Hispanic white households fell in real terms between 1989 and 1992, that of nonwhite and Hispanic households increased in real terms.

The mean financial wealth of nonwhite and Hispanic households also gained on non-Hispanic whites, with the ratio rising steadily from 0.18 in 1983 to 0.29 in 1992. Moreover, while real mean financial wealth fell for non-Hispanic white households between 1989 and 1992, it increased for nonwhite and Hispanic households. However, the story is different for median financial wealth. Median financial wealth for nonwhite and Hispanic households remained at virtually zero during the period 1983 to 1992. In other words, excluding housing, the average household in this group did not manage to accumulate any savings.

The homeownership rate has also shown a substantial rise for nonwhite and Hispanic households, from 44 percent in 1983 to 49 percent in 1992. In contrast, the homeownership rate among non--Hispanic white households increased by only 1 percentage point, from 68 to 69 percent. As a result, the ratio in homeownership rates has converged to 0.71 in 1992, up from 0.64 in 1983. Moreover, the percentage of nonwhite and Hispanic households with zero or negative net worth fell over the period, from 33 percent in 1983 to 31 percent in 1992, while the percentage of non-Hispanic white households with zero or negative net worth increased from 11.3 to 13.8 percent.

FAMILY INCOME AND WEALTH BY RACE AND ETHNICITY
1983, 1989, AND 1992[a]

	Mean Values			Median Values		
	Non-Hispanic Whites	Hispanics & Nonwhites[b]	Ratio	Non-Hispanic Whites	Hispanics & Nonwhites[b]	Ratio

1. *Income*

1982	43,867	25,736	0.59	30,860	18,736	0.61
1988	50,344	28,794	0.57	34,300	19,940	0.58
1991	47,746	27,809	0.58	29,413	18,852	0.64

2. *Net Worth*

1983	213,815	52,273	0.24	61,580	5,501	0.09
1989	273,217	79,328	0.29	74,966	8,598	0.11
1992	265,105	83,555	0.33	62,065	12,206	0.20

3. *Financial Wealth*

1983	157,541	27,858	0.18	17,121	51	0.00
1989	211,461	52,118	0.25	23,253	(10)	0.00
1992	199,908	58,152	0.29	19,462	220	0.01

4. *Homeownership Rate [percent]*

1983	68.1	43.6	0.64
1989	69.3	43.3	0.63
1992	69.0	48.9	0.71

5. *Percent of Households with Zero or Negative Net Worth*

1983	11.3	33.0	2.91
1989	12.1	35.4	2.93
1992	13.8	30.7	2.22

a. Source: own computations from the 1983, 1989, and 1992 Surveys of Consumer Finances. The second category includes Hispanics, blacks, American Indians, and Asians.

The results thus show that nonwhite and Hispanic households have continued to make gains on non-Hispanic white households in terms of wealth over the period from 1983 to 1992. However, what is still disturbing is that even in 1992, the wealth of nonwhite and Hispanic households averaged only one third that of non-Hispanic white households, in contrast to an income ratio of about 60 percent. Moreover, the ratio in medians was 64 percent for income and only 20 percent for *wealth*. Median financial wealth among nonwhite and Hispanic households was still virtually zero in 1992 and the percent with zero or negative net worth was still above 30 percent, in contrast to 14 percent among non-Hispanic white households (a difference that appears to mirror the gap in poverty rates). Thus, even though there have been some gains in closing the racial wealth gap, in 1992 it still remained far greater than the income gap.

CONCLUDING COMMENTS

There is both good news and bad news provided in this update. The good news is that there was a slight remission in wealth inequality found between 1989 and 1992. The share of the top 1 percent of wealth holders fell by almost two percentage points, and the Gini coefficient declined by 0.017. The bad news is that the dramatic rise in wealth inequality previously reported for the period 1983-89 was not entirely reversed during the early 1990s, as some studies have indicated. The share of the top 1 percent of wealth holders was still 3.4 percentage points greater in 1992 than in 1983 and the difference in Gini coefficients was 0.024. Median wealth (in 1992 dollars) was lower in 1992 than in 1983, and the bottom three quintiles saw their average real wealth decline. Over the period from 1983 to 1992, the top 20 percent of wealth holders received 99 percent of the total gain in wealth and the top 1 percent 58 percent of wealth growth. Results are disturbingly similar for financial wealth.

Income inequality, after rising dramatically between 1983 and 1989, stabilized between 1989 and 1992. However, there was a drop in both mean and median real income between 1989 and 1992. Indeed, between 1983 and 1992, the bottom 80 percent of households, as ranked in terms of income, suffered an absolute decline in their average real income. Only the top 20 percent saw their incomes rise over the period. Between 1983 and 1992, over 100 percent of the growth of income went into the hands of the top 20 percent of income recipients and almost two thirds to the top 1 percent.

Another piece of good news is that the gains made by nonwhite and Hispanic households relative to non-Hispanic white households in terms of wealth holdings between 1983 and 1989 continued into the early 1990s. The ratio of mean net worth increased from 0.24 in 1983 to 0.33 in 1992, the ratio of median net worth from 0.09 to 0.20, and the ratio of mean financial wealth from 0.18 to 0.29. The homeownership rate among nonwhite and Hispanic households continued to climb, from 44 percent in 1983 to 49 percent in 1992.

However, even by 1992, the wealth of the average (median) nonwhite and Hispanic household averaged only 20 percent that of the median non-Hispanic white household, in contrast to an income ratio of 64 percent. Median financial wealth among nonwhite and Hispanic households still remained at just about zero in 1992 and the percent with no positive net worth was still above 30 percent.

Another disturbing trend is the growing indebtedness of the American family. The ratio of total debt to total assets among all households rose from 13 percent in 1983 to 15 percent in 1992. Net equity in owner-occupied housing as a share of total assets fell sharply over this period, from 24 to 19 percent, reflecting rising mortgage debt on homeowner's property. Moreover, the proportion of households without positive net worth climbed from 15.5 percent in 1983 to 18.3 percent in 1992.

Investment-type assets remained as concentrated in the hands of the rich in 1992 as in 1989. In the two years, the richest 10 percent of families in terms of wealth owned about 90 percent of all the stock shares, bonds, trusts, and business equity, and over 80 percent of the non-home real estate of households.

These results suggest some of the sources of the growing anxiety of the middle class in this country over the last decade and a half. Between 1983 and 1992, real incomes have fallen for all households except the top 20 percent of the income distribution. Median net worth has also fallen. Median financial wealth was the same in 1992 as in 1983—still only $10,000. The average indebtedness of American families relative to their assets continued to rise between 1983 and 1992, as did mortgage debt on the value of owner-occupied housing. There has been almost no trickle down of economic growth to the average family: almost all the growth in household income and wealth has accrued to the richest 20 percent. The finances of the average American family are more fragile in the 1990s than in the early 1980s. It is not surprising that there is a growing sense of economic insecurity in the country.

DEFINING AND MEASURING WEALTH

DEFINITIONS OF WEALTH

This study uses three basic concepts of wealth: marketable wealth, "augmented wealth," and financial wealth.

Marketable wealth (or net worth), HW, is the current value of all marketable or fungible assets ("fungible" ones are defined as liquid assets plus stocks and other equities) less the current value of debts. Total assets are defined as the sum of: (1) the gross value of owner-occupied housing; (2) other real estate owned by the household; (3) cash and demand deposits; (4) time and savings deposits, certificates of deposit, and money market accounts; (5) government bonds, corporate bonds, foreign bonds, and other financial securities; (6) the cash surrender value of life insurance plans; (7) the cash surrender value of pension plans, including IRAs and Keogh plans; (8) corporate stock, including mutual funds; (9) net equity in unincorporated businesses; and (10) equity in trust funds. Total liabilities are the sum of: (1) mortgage debt, (2) consumer debt, and (3) other debt.

This first measure of wealth is used because the primary interest here is in wealth as a store of value and therefore a source of potential consumption. This is the concept that best reflects the level of well-being associated with a family's holdings. Thus, only assets that can be readily converted to cash are included.

A somewhat expanded variant of the first measure is HWX, which is defined as the sum of HW and consumer durables. Consumer durables include automobiles, televisions, furniture, household appliances, and the like. Although these items provide consumption services directly to the household, they are not easily marketed. In fact, the resale value of these items typically far understates the value of their consumption services to the household. However, this concept is useful for consistency with earlier studies, in particular, for the construction of a long-term time-series for the United States.[1]

A wider definition of household wealth will often add some valuation of pension rights, from both public and private sources, to marketable wealth. One of the major developments in the postwar period among industrialized countries has been the enormous growth in both public and private pension systems. Even though such pension funds are not in the direct control of individuals or families, they are a source of future income to families and thus may be perceived as a form of family wealth. Moreover, as Martin Feldstein has argued, insofar as families accumulate "traditional" wealth to provide for future consumption needs, the growth of such pension funds may have offset private savings and hence traditional wealth accumulation.[2] Such a measure may thus provide a better gauge of potential future consumption.

The second major concept used here is "augmented wealth," AW, defined as the sum of household wealth HW, pension wealth, and Social Security wealth.[3] Pension wealth is defined as the present value of discounted future pension benefits. In similar fashion, Social Security wealth is defined as the present value of the discounted stream of future Social Security benefits. A variant of AW is AWX, defined as the sum of HWX and retirement (pension and Social Security) wealth. This concept is also employed for consistency with earlier studies.[4]

The third concept is financial wealth, FW, defined as net worth minus net equity in owner-occupied housing (the difference between the value of the property and its outstanding mortgage debt). Financial wealth is a more "liquid" concept than marketable wealth, since one's home is difficult to convert into cash in the short term. It thus reflects the resources that may be directly available for consumption or various forms of investments.

DATA AND MEASUREMENT

Data on the size distribution of household wealth in the United States are available principally from estate tax records and cross-sectional household surveys. The existing information can be pieced together to document the historical trends. A reasonably consistent series of estate tax records for the very wealthy collected nationally exists for selected years between 1922 and 1986. Comparative estimates of household wealth inequality are also provided from four surveys conducted by the Federal Reserve Board, in 1962, 1983, 1986 (a special follow-up of the 1983 survey), and 1989. As indicated above, these are based on stratified samples and are reasonably consistent over time.[5] In addition, a figure for 1979 is obtained from the Income Survey and Development Program (ISDP) of that year.

MARKETABLE WEALTH

·   There are three principal sets of studies that have constructed time-series from these data. The first, by Robert Lampman, covers the years from 1922 through 1953[6]; the second, by James D. Smith, provides concentration figures for the period from 1953 to 1976[7]; and the third, by Edward N. Wolff and Marcia Marley, constructs new estimates for the 1922–81 period.[8] The Lampman data and the Smith data are each internally consistent, using the same accounting conventions and the same set of national balance sheet estimates throughout. The Wolff-Marley study provides a consistent accounting framework and consistent set of national balance sheet totals in order to reconcile the Lampman and Smith estimates.

Table A–1 (pages 62–63) shows the original results of the Wolff-Marley series. These estimates are based on the Lampman data, which cover the period from 1922 to 1953, and the Smith results, covering 1953 to 1976. The estate files used by Lampman and Smith do not include all assets, and the authors used different assumptions concerning pensions and trusts.[9] Another asset, life insurance, is overstated in the estate files (since it is reckoned at its face value rather than its cash surrender value), a problem that both Lampman and Smith appreciated and made adjustments for. Another difference is that Lampman's concentration estimates are based on estimates of aggregate household wealth prepared by Raymond W. Goldsmith,[10] while Smith's estimates used aggregate data from Richard and Nancy Ruggles.[11]

In order to derive a more consistent series on household wealth concentration, Wolff and Marley made a series of adjustments to the Lampman and Smith figures. First, they used consistent aggregate household balance sheet totals to derive the concentration estimates. Second, imputations were provided for the assets that were left out of the estate files, particularly trusts, and estimates of pensions and insurance values

Table A-1

Percentage Share of Total Marketable Household Wealth Held By the Richest 1 Percent of Wealth Holders in the United States, 1922-1989[a]

Year	Wolff-Marley Series[b]			Other Sources[c]		New Series Households	
	Individuals		Households	Households			
	Total Assets	Net Worth	Total Assets	Total Assets	Net Worth	Net Worth (HWX)	Augmented Wealth (AWX)[d]
1922	34.0		25.5			36.7	34.3
1929	37.2		30.7			44.2	41.1
1933	31.3					33.3	28.7
1939	38.1		25.3			36.4	30.2
1945	28.9		20.7			29.8	22.0
1949	25.7		18.8			27.1	20.7
1953	28.1	28.4	21.7			31.2	23.1
1958	27.0	27.7	20.0	28.8	20.4		
1962	30.1	31.1	22.1	29.9	31.8	31.8	21.9

TABLE A–1 (CONTINUED)

PERCENTAGE SHARE OF TOTAL MARKETABLE
HOUSEHOLD WEALTH HELD BY THE RICHEST 1 PERCENT
OF WEALTH HOLDERS IN THE UNITED STATES, 1922–1989[a]

| | WOLFF-MARLEY SERIES[b] | | | OTHER SOURCES[c] | | NEW SERIES HOUSEHOLDS | |
| | INDIVIDUALS | | HOUSEHOLDS | HOUSEHOLDS | | | |
YEAR	TOTAL ASSETS	NET WORTH	TOTAL ASSETS	TOTAL ASSETS	NET WORTH	NET WORTH (HWX)	AUGMENTED WEALTH (AWX)[d]
1965	31.9	33.6	23.9			34.4	23.3
1969	29.0	30.2	21.6		30.8	31.1	20.9
1972	28.6	29.8	20.2			29.1	19.0
1976	18.9	19.1	12.7			19.9	13.3
1979					20.5	20.5	12.9
1981	23.6					24.8	15.5
1983					30.9	30.9	19.0
1986					31.9	31.9	19.3
1989					35.7	35.7	21.2

Notes on page 64.

Notes to Table A–1

a. The concept used here is marketable wealth, including consumer durables (HWX).

b. *Source*: Wolff and Marley (1989), Tables 5, 6, 7, and 8. The results are based on the "W2" series, which is comparable to HWX. Figures on the share of assets owned by the top 1 percent of households (column 3) are lower-bound estimates.

c. *Sources*: 1962, from the *Survey of Financial Characteristics of Consumers;* 1969 from Wolff (1983), based on the MESP database; 1979, from Radner and Vaughan (1987), based on the Income Survey and Development Program (ISDP), where the share of wealth of the top 1 percent of households is estimated using a Pareto distribution; 1983, 1986, and 1989 from the *Survey of Consumer Finances.*

d. *Source*: Wolff and Marley (1989), Table 6. The results are based on the "W4" series, where W4 is defined as marketable wealth (W2) plus pension reserves and social security wealth.

were standardized. Moreover, an additional data point was added to the series for 1981 on the basis of a study by Marvin Schwartz.[12]

The first column of Table A–1 shows the resulting series for the share of total assets held by the top 1 percent of asset owners and the second column for the share of net worth owned by the top 1 percent of wealth holders. The wealth concept used here is marketable wealth including consumer durables (HWX). Concentration figures are slightly higher based on net worth rather than on total assets, since relative indebtedness (the debt-equity ratio) is higher for poorer individuals than richer ones.[13]

The estate files represent the wealth of the deceased. The wealth estimates for the living population are derived using the estate multiplier method, which divides the population by age and sex and weights the deceased from each group as registered by the estate files by the reciprocal of the survival probability for that group. The survival probabilities used are higher than those for the population at large, due to the longer expected life span of the wealthy. This method represents a point estimate that can have a very large variance, particularly for the young, since there are very few of them in the sample. Estate estimates have been criticized by A. B. Atkinson and A. F. Shorrocks as overestimating the decline in inequality.[14] The reason is that estate estimates are based on the individual rather than the household unit, and over the century marital customs and relations have changed. Married women now inherit more wealth and have higher wealth levels than they did in 1900 or 1930. This reduces the individual concentration even if household wealth inequality does not change. For example, between 1929 and 1953, Lampman reported that the percentage of married women among the top wealth holders increased from 9 to 18 percent.

Column 3 of Table A–1 shows the estimates of the share of total assets owned by the top 1 percent of *households*. As mentioned, estate files record wealth for the individual, while the more interesting unit for welfare analysis is the household. Moreover, the increased tendency to divide wealth equally between household members will reduce the individual concentration estimates without changing household wealth concentration. In order to change the estate data to a household base, certain assumptions are required about the division of wealth within households. The series shown in column 3 of Table A–1 is based upon the set of assumptions that yielded the smallest concentration estimates.[15] A comparison of columns 1 and 3 indicates that concentration figures are considerably lower on the basis of the household unit than the individual unit. This is to be expected since a married couple typically mixes a relatively affluent spouse with a less wealthy one. Estimates from six other sources of wealth data are shown in the next two columns. These are all based on the household as the unit of observation. Three sources—the 1962 *Survey of Financial Characteristics of Consumers* (SFCC), the 1983 *Survey of Consumer Finances* (SCF), and the 1989 SCF—were conducted under the auspices of the Federal Reserve Board and include a high-income supplement. Imputations were made for missing values, and each sample has been aligned to the national balance sheet totals for that year to ensure greater consistency.[16]

The 1969 figure is derived from the MESP file, a synthetic database that is also fully aligned to the national balance sheet totals of that year.[17] The 1979 figure is based on the Daniel B. Radner and Denton R. Vaughan calculations from the 1979 ISDP,[18] which have then been benchmarked to the 1969 figure on the basis of a Pareto interpolation. Estimates are also available from the 1986 SCF, which resurveyed the families included in the 1983 SCF sample. Though there was a substantial "dropout rate" among the survey respondents, research by Robert B. Avery and Arthur B. Kennickell does provide some comparative estimates of wealth concentration in the two years.[19] The seven figures shown in column 5 of Table A–1 are all relatively consistent.

To combine column 5 with the Wolff-Marley series, an overlapping year is necessary. Fortunately, two such "Rosetta stones" are provided, for 1962 and 1969. A comparison of columns 3 and 4 for 1962 reveals that the share of total assets owned by the top 1 percent of *households* is estimated to be considerably higher on the basis of the SFCC (29.9 percent) than on the basis of the estate tax series (22.1 percent). One possible reason for this difference is the conservative assumption used in converting the estate data to a household base. If it was instead assumed that all married men in the estate sample of top wealth holders had wedded women with wealth, the concentration estimates would have been higher, but not enough to account for the difference.[20] Another likely reason for the discrepancy between the estate and survey estimates is that there may be a serious underreporting problem in the estate data.[21]

Column 6 of Table A–1 shows the new series for the share of net worth owned by the top 1 percent of households from 1922 to 1989. Figures for the years 1962, 1969, 1979, 1983, 1986, and 1989 are based on the survey data sources. Other years, with the exception of 1933 and 1981, are calculated as the product of column 3 multiplied by the ratio of the 1962 SFCC figure for the share of household net worth in column 5 (31.8 percent) and the estate tax figure for the share of household assets in column 3 (22.1 percent)—a ratio of 1.44. A similar procedure applied to the 1969 data yields almost the same ratio (1.43), which provides some confidence in this benchmarking procedure. Figures for 1933 and 1981 are interpolated on the basis of column 1.

The estimates of the "New Series" in column 6 show a high concentration of wealth throughout the period from 1922 to 1989. A quarter or more of total wealth was owned by the top 1 percent in each of these years except 1976 and 1981. A comparison of the two end points reveals almost identical concentration figures: 36.7 percent in 1922 and 35.7 percent in 1989. However, this comparison hides important trends over the period.

Between 1922 and 1929 there was a substantial increase in wealth concentration, from 37 to 44 percent (also see Figure 3–1). Wealth inequality in 1929 was at a high point (and probably at its peak for the twentieth century). The Great Depression saw a sizable drop in inequality, with the share of the top percentile falling to 33 percent, but by 1939 the concentration level was almost the same as it was in 1922.

There followed a substantial drop in inequality between 1939 and 1945, a result of the leveling effects of World War II, and a more modest decline between 1945 and 1949.

The share of wealth held by the richest 1 percent of households showed a gradual upward trend from 27 percent in 1949 to a peak of 34 percent in 1965. There followed a rather pronounced fall in wealth inequality lasting until 1979. Between 1965 and 1972, the share of the top percentile fell from 34 to 29 percent, and then from 29 to 20 percent between 1972 and 1976.[22] The main reason for the decline in concentration over this four-year period is the sharp drop in the value of corporate stock held by the top wealth holders. The total value of corporate stock owned by the richest 1 percent fell from $491 billion in 1972 to $297 billion in 1976.[22] Moreover, this decline appears to be attributable to the steep decline in share prices rather than a divestiture of stock holdings.

Wealth inequality appears to have bottomed out some time during the late 1970s. A sharp increase in wealth concentration occurred between 1979 and 1981, from a 21 to a 25 percent share; again from 1981 to 1983, from a 24 to a 31 percent share; and then once more between 1983 and 1989, from 31 to 36 percent. This sharp rise in the concentration of household wealth paralleled the growth in income inequality evident during the 1980s.[24]

RETIREMENT WEALTH

The last column of Table A–1 shows the "New Series" for the share of augmented household wealth, AWX (including consumer durables), owned by the top 1 percent of wealth holders. A similar procedure is used to develop this series as was done for HWX. The original source is the Wolff-Marley W4 series, where W4 is defined to include full pension reserves, which are reported in the aggregate data sources, as well as imputations for Social Security wealth.[25] However, one major difficulty is that there is very little information concerning the percentage of total pensions owned by the top wealth holders. In the Wolff-Marley paper, alternative assumptions were made about this share, ranging from a maximum of 15 percent to a minimum of 3 percent for the top 1 percent of wealth holders. The different assumptions had little effect on total wealth concentration. In the estimates reported for W4, it was assumed that the share of total pension wealth held by the top percentile of wealth holders declined over the course of the twentieth century because of the increase of pension coverage throughout the period.

Direct imputations of pension and Social Security wealth were made for the 1962 SFCC, the 1969 MESP, the 1983 SCF, and the 1989 SCF microdata files.[26] These estimates were used for the "New Series" for AWX shown in column 7.[27] Figures for W4 from 1922 through 1976 were then benchmarked against the 1962 estimate derived from the SFCC. Other years were filled in by interpolation.

The addition of pension and Social Security wealth has had a significant effect on measured wealth inequality (also see Figure 3–1). Because of the growth over time in pension and Social Security wealth, particularly the latter, in relation to marketable wealth, the gap between the HWX and the AWX series widens over time, from two percentage points in 1922 to thirteen percentage points in 1989. However, the time patterns are almost identical. Wealth concentration based on the AWX series showed a sharp increase between 1922 and 1929; a substantial decline from 1929 to 1933; an increase between 1933 and 1939; a significant decrease between 1939 and 1945; a fairly flat trend from 1945 through 1972; a sharp decline from 1972 to 1976; and then a substantial rise between 1979 and 1989. The increase on the basis of augmented wealth during the 1980s, eight percentage points, appears more muted than the comparable figure for marketable wealth, fifteen percentage points.

METHODOLOGICAL NOTES ON THE MEASUREMENT OF WEALTH

In most industrialized countries today, there are now official estimates of the size distribution of household income. In the United States, for example, the Census Bureau conducts an annual survey in March, called the *Current Population Survey*, which provides detailed information on individual and household earnings and income. On the basis of these data, the U.S. Census Bureau constructs its estimates of both family and household income inequality. Moreover, the *Current Population Survey* has been conducted in the United States ever since 1947. As a result, there exists a consistent time-series on household income distribution for the United States that covers more than forty-six years.

Unfortunately, there do not exist comparable data on the size distribution of household wealth for the United States or, for that matter, for any other country in the world. There are no official household surveys conducted on an annual basis for this purpose. As a result, researchers in this field have had to make estimates of household wealth inequality from a variety of sources, which are often inconsistent. Compounding this problem is the fact that household wealth is much more heavily concentrated in the upper percentiles of the distribution than is income. Thus, unless surveys or data sources are especially designed to cover the top wealth groups in a country, it is easy to produce biased estimates of the size distribution of wealth. The end result is that estimates of household wealth distribution are less reliable than those for income distribution.

There are correspondingly many more methodological problems associated with household wealth data than with income data. These include: asset coverage, the unit of observation, underreporting, sampling frame, and institutional differences in wealth ownership over time. Estimates of the size distribution of household wealth are quite sensitive to each of these considerations. As a result, it is precarious to compare inequality figures between different data sources. This is particularly true in making international comparisons. However, it is still possible to develop time trends on the basis of a single data source and to combine such time trends if benchmark estimates are available for the same years.

The principal data sources on household wealth will be described first in order to see how these considerations come into play. There have been five such sources: estate tax data, household survey data, wealth tax data, income capitalization techniques, and synthetic data sources. Each has its characteristic advantages and disadvantages.

ESTATE TAX DATA

Estate tax data was the first major source of data used for wealth analysis. Estate tax records are actual tax returns filed for probate. Such data have a great degree of reliability, since they are subject to scrutiny and audit by the state. Their main limitation, in the United States at least, is that the threshold for filing is relatively high, so that only a small proportion of estates (typically, 1 percent or so) are required to file returns.[28] Another difficulty with these data is that the sample consists of decedents. As a result, various assumptions must be used to construct "estate multipliers" in order to infer the distribution of wealth among the living. Insofar as mortality rates are inversely correlated with wealth (that is, the rich tend to live longer), the resulting multipliers can be biased. Moreover, the resulting estimated distribution of wealth is by individual rather than by family. Changing ownership patterns within families (for example, joint ownership of the family's house) can affect estimated wealth concentration. In addition, various other assumptions must be made to infer family wealth from estimates of individual wealth holdings.

Another problem involves underreporting and nonfiling for tax avoidance. Though the returns are subject to audit, the value of cash on hand, jewelry, housewares, and business assets is difficult to ascertain. Their value is typically understated in order to reduce the tax liability of the estate. Moreover, inter vivos transfers (that is, gifts between living individuals), particularly in anticipation of death, can bias estimates of household wealth among the living.[29]

HOUSEHOLD SURVEY DATA

The second principal source is the field survey. Its primary advantage is that it provides considerable discretion to the interviewer about the information requested of respondents. However, the major drawback is that information provided by the respondent is often inaccurate, and, in many cases, the information requested is not provided at all. Another problem is that because household wealth is extremely skewed, the very rich (the so-called upper tail of the distribution) are often considerably underrepresented in samples. During the 1980s, the two major wealth surveys for the United States constructed on the basis of a representative sample have been the 1984 and 1988 *Survey of Income and Program Participation* (SIPP).[30]

An alternative is to use stratified samples, based typically on income tax returns, which oversample the rich. However, studies indicate that response error and nonresponse rates are considerably higher among the wealthy than among the middle class. Moreover, there are problems in "weighting" the sample in order to reflect the actual population distribution. There have, to date, been three major stratified samples for the United States, all conducted by the Federal Reserve Board.[31]

To give a sense of how much difference the choice of sampling frame makes in estimating wealth concentration, it is instructive to calculate the Gini coefficient (a standard measure of the concentration of wealth) from the 1983 and 1989 *Survey of Consumer Finances* (SCF) and from the 1984 and 1988 *Survey of Income and Program Participation* files. The results are as follows:

GINI COEFFICIENT OF HOUSEHOLD WEALTH DISTRIBUTION

1983 SCF	0.80
1984 SIPP	0.69
1988 SIPP	0.69
1989 SCF	0.84

The measured concentration is substantially higher on the basis of the stratified SCF files than on the basis of the representative SIPP files.[32] In general, the greater the coverage of the upper wealth groups in a sample, the higher is the degree of measured wealth concentration. As a result, one must remain rather suspicious of wealth inequality figures based on representative samples.[33]

WEALTH TAX DATA

A third source is wealth tax return data. A dozen or so European countries, including Germany, the Netherlands, and Sweden, assess taxes not only on current income but also on the stock of household wealth (see Chapter 8 for more details). Though there is typically a threshold for paying wealth taxes, their coverage of the population can be considerably greater than that of estate tax returns. However, the measurement problems are similar to those of estate tax data. The filer has a great incentive to understate the value of the family's assets, or even not to report them. Moreover, the assets subject to tax do not cover the full range of household assets (for example, consumer durables are often excluded). In addition, the observational unit of measurement is the tax filing, which does not directly correspond to the family unit. Wealth tax data have been used extensively by Roland Spånt for an analysis of wealth trends in Sweden.[34]

INCOME CAPITALIZATION TECHNIQUES

The fourth type of wealth data is based on "income capitalization" techniques, which are usually applied to income tax return data. In this procedure, certain income flows, such as dividends, rents, and interest, are converted into corresponding asset values based on the average asset yield. For example, dividends are capitalized in order to estimate corporate stock holdings. This method also suffers from a number of defects. First, only assets with a corresponding income flow are covered in this procedure. Thus, owner-occupied housing, consumer durables, and idle land cannot be directly captured. Also, in the United States, state and local bonds cannot be estimated because their interest income is exempt from federal income taxes. Second, the estimation procedure rests heavily on the assumption that asset yields are uncorrelated with asset levels. Any actual correlation between the size of asset holdings and yields can produce biased estimates. Third, the observational unit is again based on the tax return. Various assumptions must be imposed in order to construct family wealth estimates from those of the tax filer. Charles Stewart conducted the earliest study on U.S. data using this technique.[35]

SYNTHETIC DATA SOURCES

Another source of wealth data involves combining two or more basic sources of data, as well as the merging and matching of data sets. There are two principal examples of this approach for the United States. Edward N. Wolff statistically matched 1969 U.S. tax return data from the Internal Revenue Service with the 1970 U.S. Census of Population survey data. Income capitalization was then applied to the tax return data to obtain the values of corresponding assets, and the census data were used to supply values for some of the missing assets, such as the value of owner-occupied housing.[36] Daphne T. Greenwood used a specially constructed data set in which individual income tax records were matched to family records in the 1973 *Current Population Survey*. Income capitalization was also applied to income flows to obtain corresponding asset values.[37] This approach has the advantage of combining the strengths of the basic data sources. However, the major pitfall is that the joint distributions of noncommon variables in the two data sources, inferred from statistical matches, are statistically unreliable.

NOTES

➤ 1

1. U.S. Council of Economic Advisers (1994).

➤ 2

1. Wealth is defined formally and in detail in the Appendix. To summarize very roughly and briefly, wealth is the difference between the value of assets and liabilities; three variations of wealth are employed in this paper. *Financial* wealth includes only assets (1)–(6), below; *Marketable* wealth includes assets (1)–(10); *Augmented* wealth includes all assets listed below. "Wealth" without an adjective refers to marketable wealth. Assets include (1) cash and demand deposits; (2) time and savings deposits, certificates of deposit, and money market accounts; (3) government bonds, corporate bonds, foreign bonds, and other financial securities; (4) the cash surrender value of life insurance plans; (5) the cash surrender value of pension plans, including IRAs and Keogh plans; (6) corporate stock, including mutual funds; (7) the gross value of owner-occupied housing; (8) other real estate owned by the household; (9) net equity in unincorporated businesses; (10) equity in trust funds; (11) consumer durables; and (12) some valuation of pension rights, from both public and private sources. Total liabilities are the sum of (I) mortgage debt, (II) consumer debt, and (III) other debt.

2. Technically, there is a distinction between savings out of income, the difference between current income and current consumption, which is a national income and product account concept, and the revaluation of existing assets (capital gains and losses), which is a balance sheet concept.

3. In one attempt to explain the variation of wealth holdings by various factors, Greenwood (1987) found that income increased the amount of variation explained only from 6 to 17 percent. Wolff (1994) reported on the basis of 1989 wealth data that the inequality of wealth within income class was almost as pronounced as in the population as a whole.

4. Steuerle (1984).

5. Moreover, asset income is generally not well reported. Income statistics in the United States are generally based on census data (the *Current Population Survey*, primarily). Although coverage of wage and salary income is quite good, these data typically substantially understate property income such as dividends, interest, and rent. In some years, reported property income is less than half of what the national income and product accounts indicate it should be. It is therefore inadequate to use conventional income data to capture the distribution of asset income in this country.

6. See Radner and Vaughan (1987).

➤ 3

1. Household wealth has historically been and remains much more concentrated than household income, despite the rise in income inequality. In 1989, the top 1 percent of income recipients accounted for 16 percent of total household income, much less than the 39 percent of total wealth held by the top 1 percent of wealth holders. See, for example, the excellent review of income inequality trends by Levy and Murnane (1992).

2. Results in this section are based on the 1962 *Survey of Financial Characteristics of Consumers* (SFCC), the 1983 *Survey of Consumer Finances* (SCF), and the 1989 SCF, all fully aligned with national balance sheet data. See Wolff (1994) for technical details. Data for earlier periods are reviewed in the Appendix.

3. Distributions of wealth (and income) typically are organized into "quintiles," that is, into groups of households arranged from poorest to wealthiest. The wealthiest 20 percent may be called the "top quintile." The bottom quintile is the least wealthy 20 percent of all households. The poorest 40 percent may be referred to as the "bottom two quintiles" or as the "bottom quintile and the next quintile."

4. If everyone were to receive a dollar increase in wealth, then the mean and median both would increase by a dollar as well. If the same total increase in wealth were enjoyed by the wealthiest person alone, average (mean) wealth still would rise by a dollar but the median would remain unchanged.

5. Median financial wealth also grew more slowly in both periods than mean financial wealth, but its growth increased from 0.6 percent per year in the 1962–83 period to 2.5 percent per year in the 1983–89 period. Median household income, like median financial wealth, grew faster in 1983–89 (at 1.2 percent per year) than in 1962–83 (0.8 percent per year). In both periods, the growth in median income was less than that of median (and mean) wealth.

6. Please note that these figures differ from the "New Series" in Table 4–1, since the latter are based on HWX (see Appendix) which includes consumer durables.

7. It should be noted that the concentration of income figures reported here on the basis of the 1983 and 1989 SCF are considerably higher than those based on the U.S. Census *Current Population Surveys* (CPS), noted in Chapter 6. This is not surprising for two reasons. First, the SCF has a high-income supplement and therefore provides better coverage of rich families than does the CPS (see Appendix for explanation of methodology). Second, the CPS "top-codes" income entries at $100,000 (the highest income interval is "$100,000 or more"), thus understating the income of the richest families, whereas the SCF has no top coding.

8. It should be noted that in these calculations, the households found in each group (say, the top quintile) may be different in the two years due to economic mobility.

➤ **4**

1. Families are classified into age group on the basis of the age of the family head.

2. See Modigliani and Brumberg (1954) for a discussion of the "life-cycle model of savings."

3. Technically, IRAs can hold any type of asset, though in 1989 they were predominantly in the form of bank deposits.

4. A similar trend is evident for the Census's home ownership rate, which increased from 55.0 percent in 1950 to a peak of 64.6 percent in 1975 but subsequently declined to 63.5 percent in 1985.

➤ **5**

1. Several problems with the estate data source and methodology for the United Kingdom are discussed by Shorrocks (1987). First, the estate multiplier method is likely to lead to some bias in estimated wealth shares because of the

positive correlation between wealth and life expectancy (wealthier individuals tend to live longer). Second, the value of household goods and small businesses are likely to be understated in estate data, since their value is considerably greater when in use than when put up for sale. Third, the value of life insurance policies is considerably greater in estates, since they are fully paid out, than comparable policies in the hands of the living. Fourth, except for life insurance policies, the total value of assets based on estate tax data falls far short of national balance sheet figures for the household sector.

2. The U.S. series is based on HWX for household unit. See the Appendix and notes to Table 4–1 for sources and methods for the United States. Sources for the United Kingdom are: 1923–75—Shorrocks (1987), Tables 2.1 and 2.2; 1976–90—Board of Inland Revenue (1992), Series C, Table 11.5. Results are based on marketable wealth for adult individuals. The 1923–75 data are benchmarked to the Inland Revenue series. Sources for Sweden are: 1920–75—Spånt (1987), Tables 3.7, 3.8, and 3.11; 1975–90—Statistics Sweden (1992), Table 49. The unit is the household; wealth is valued at market prices. The 1920–75 data are benchmarked to the Statistics Sweden series.

3. See Kessler and Wolff (1991) for details.

4. The French data come from the 1986 Enquête sur les Actifs Financiers conducted by the Institut National de la Statistique et des Etudes Economiques (INSEE). The sample size is 5,602 families. This survey has a rather complex design, which is stratified by various sociodemographic characteristics. However, there is no special stratification by high income.

For the United States, the 1983 *Survey of Consumer Finances* (SCF), conducted by the Federal Reserve Board, is used. The 1983 SCF has a sample size of 4,262 families. Of these, 3,824 were randomly drawn and thus constitute a representative sample. The remaining 438 families constitute the so-called high-income supplement. These families were selected on the basis of their high income from a special sample created by the Internal Revenue Service from income tax returns. The U.S. survey data were then adjusted to conform to the coverage of the French survey data. Automobiles and other consumer durables were eliminated from the U.S. data, since these assets are not captured in the French data. Moreover, since household debt is not covered in the French survey, statistics are shown for total assets instead of net worth.

5. There are two other possible explanations of the differences. The first is that there are differences in the degree of underreporting of assets in the two surveys. In other words, if holdings of particular assets by households are not accurately reported, this will distort the measured inequality from survey data. It proved feasible to check the potential bias for the U.S. survey data by aligning the U.S. survey data to national balance sheet totals. See Wolff (1987a) for details.

The second possible explanation is that the sampling frame differs between the two surveys. In particular, the U.S. data have a special component of high-income households that does not exist in the French data. It is well known that the better the coverage of high-income households, the higher is measured wealth inequality from such a survey. Thus, part of the reason for the finding of greater wealth inequality in the United States than in France may be the greater coverage of wealthy families in the U.S. data.

6. See O'Higgins, Schmaus, and Stephenson (1989), Table 2, for example.

➤ 6

1. The basic data source is the *Current Population Report* series on shares of income held by families that runs from 1947 to 1989. The earlier data, from 1922 to 1949, are from Kuznets's (1953) series on the percentage share of total income received by the top percentiles of tax units. This series is benchmarked against the census figure for 1949.

2. The source for the income data in this section is U.S. Bureau of the Census (1990c), p. 30. Results are based on the household unit, including families and unrelated individuals. Statistics on family income alone, available from the same source, show almost identical trends.

3. Incomes of poor households have not fallen only because these households have worked more hours, as more women have joined the work force. Women's wages have been rising, but men with less than a college education saw their real wages drop substantially in the 1980s.

4. This argument would not apply as readily to augmented household wealth (AW), since pension reserves are held mainly in the form of corporate stock shares and pension wealth is more widespread in the population than individual ownership of corporate stock. Moreover, even in the case of marketable wealth, which includes the surrender value of many types of defined contribution plans (steadily displacing defined benefit plans in private pensions over the last decade or so), the marketable wealth of middle-class families will be increasingly subject to fluctuations in the stock market.

5. A straightforward regression of a wealth inequality index, measured by the share of marketable wealth held by the top 1 percent of households (WLTH) on income inequality, measured by the share of income received by the top 5 percent of families (INC), and the ratio of stock prices (the Standard and Poor index) to housing prices (RATIO), with eighteen data readings between 1922 and 1989, yields:

$$WLTH = 4.50 + 1.17\,INC + 1.04\,RATIO, \quad R2 = 0.62, \quad N = 18$$
$$(0.8) \quad (3.8) \quad\quad\quad (2.3)$$

with t-ratios shown in parentheses. Both variables are statistically significant (INC at the 1 percent level and RATIO at the 5 percent level) and with the expected (positive) sign. Also, the fit is quite good, even for this simple model. The dominant factor in explaining changes in wealth concentration is income inequality. However, the movement in the ratio of stock to housing prices explains most of the increase in wealth inequality between 1949 and 1965 and the subsequent decline between 1965 and 1979 (particularly between 1972 and 1976). What about the 1980s? From the regression results, almost half (49 percent) of the increase in wealth concentration between 1981 and 1989 is attributable to the increase in income inequality and 21 percent to the increase of stock prices relative to housing prices.

➤ 7

1. A related tax is the property tax, levied on the value of all real property (buildings and land). Though this is often overlooked in current debates on tax reforms, the property tax is the third-largest source of household tax revenue and has been rising steeply in recent years. This tax is generally levied by local governments in this country and, as a result, will not be discussed in the present report. Of the twenty-four OECD countries, all but Italy and Portugal have a separate tax on real property.

2. Gifts within three years of death are treated as transfers at death.

3. There are some complications that arise from capital losses and the carryover of capital losses from previous years, particularly in regard to short-term capital gains.

4. Most of the information in this section is garnered from the Organization of Economic Cooperation and Development (1988). The figures in this section are as of 1988 in most cases and are, of course, subject to change over time.

5. Japan also had a direct wealth tax for a short period after World War II.

6. In Switzerland, the wealth tax is actually a provincial (canton) tax, so that provisions vary among cantons.

7. There is a technical issue related to debts on excluded assets. Since the wealth tax is based on the total value of assets *less* debts, the appropriate treatment would be to exclude debts on assets that are themselves excluded from the tax base. However, because of the difficulty of assigning specific debts (such as bank overdrafts) to specific assets, countries vary in their treatment of this problem.

8. Actually, in the U.S. estate tax system, preferential treatment is given to a spousal transfer in the form of a complete exemption. There is also a special, additional tax levied on generation-skipping bequests.

9. The source is U.S. Council of Economic Advisers (1992), p. 387.

➤ 8

1. It should be noted that in the simulations all assets are appraised at market value (since this is the only valuation available).

2. The procedure was as follows: First, adjusted gross income (AGI) was estimated as the sum of all income items (excluding Social Security income). Second, the number of exemptions was computed. Third, the standard deduction was calculated. This is based on the filing status of the household and the number of persons sixty-five or older in the household. Fourth, taxable income was calculated by taking AGI minus the number of exemptions multiplied by $2,000 and subtracting the standard deduction. Federal income tax was then computed on the basis of the appropriate tax tables. After the initial run, the estimation procedure could be calibrated. Total individual federal income taxes collected in 1989 amounted to $445.7 billion (the source is the Council of Economic Advisors [1991], Table B-77). The tax estimation used here produces a total tax figure for all households of $526.4 billion (an 18 percent discrepancy). The tax estimates were subsequently reduced by 18 percent to align with the actual figure. With this system, taxes were then recomputed in the same way, except in treating household wealth as an additional taxable item in accordance with the details of each of the three plans shown in Table 8-1.

3. Data problems include the following: (i) itemized deductions, particularly interest payments and state and local tax payments, cannot be included in the analysis; (ii) the data analysis cannot incorporate capital gains in family income; (iii) tax-exempt interest income is not excluded from AGI; and (iv) any adjustments to income are not included in the computation of AGI. It is assumed that the net effect of these omitted adjustments is approximately captured by the 18 percent adjustment to tax revenues.

4. The revenue effect estimated on the basis of the Swiss system (2.2 percent of total U.S. tax revenues) is not very far out of line with the actual experience of that country; in 1985, the Swiss wealth tax accounted for 2.3 percent of total tax revenues in Switzerland. On the other hand, the relative revenue effects estimated from the German and particularly the Swedish system are much greater than the actual wealth tax yields in those countries. There are four possible reasons for the discrepancy in results. First, total tax revenues are a higher proportion of GNP in Germany (37 percent in 1988) and in Sweden (55 percent) than in the United States (30 percent). Second, household wealth holdings relative to income may be lower in Germany and Sweden than in the United States. Third, there may be substantial tax evasion and avoidance in the two European countries. Fourth, in the case of Sweden at least, there is a cap on the joint income and wealth tax, which lim-

its liability for the wealth tax for a large proportion of wealthy Swedish families because of the very high marginal tax rates on income that existed in the 1980's.

5. However, as indicated in the previus note, the incorporation of itemized deductions, tax preference items, and other income adjustments would make the effective tax rates on income considerably less progressive.

➤ 9

1. See David (1973) for such proposal for the United States and Tait (1967) for the United Kingdom.

2. The ceiling was actually raised to $100,000 in 1926 but then lowered back to $50,000 in 1932.

3. Organization for Economic Cooperation and Development (1992). Technically, the savings rates are for the sector grouping households, nonprofit institutions, and unincorporated businesses. The sample of countries includes all those listed in Table 7-1 except Denmark, Iceland, Ireland, Luxembourg, and Turkey.

4. Other, more subtle exclusions may be warranted as well. For example, provisions to protect old people, living with low income in valuable family homes appear worthwhile. The law could, for example, postpone taxes on this wealth, incorporating them into estate taxes.

5. Greenwood and Wolff (1992), with updated estimates.

➤ POSTSCRIPT

1. It should be noted at the outset that there appears to be a substantial change in the sampling frame used in the new 1992 Survey in comparison to the 1989 Survey. For consistency with the earlier results, I have adjusted the "weights" used in the 1992 Survey of Consumer Finances. The problem can be seen most easily in the table on the following page.

A comparison of weights used in the 1989 and 1992 SCF shows a very sharp attenuation in the weights at the top of the income distribution. According to these figures, the percentage of households with incomes between $1,000,000 and $4,000,000 declined from 0.055 to 0.029, or by almost half; the percentage in the income range $4,000,000 to $7,000,000 fell from 0.013 to 0.002, or by over 80 percent; and the percentage with incomes of $7,000,000 or more decreased from 0.0049 to 0.0002, or by over 95 percent.

COMPARISON OF STATISTICS OF INCOME (SOI) AND SURVEY
OF CONSUMER FINANCES (SCF) SIZE DISTRIBUTION

Adjusted Gross Income or House-hold Income [Current $]	SCF Distribution: Percentage of All Households[a]		SOI Distribution: Percentage of All Tax Returns[b]	
	1989	1992	1989	1992
Under $100,000	95.7	94.9	97.4	96.7
100,000-199,999	3.107	3.948	1.864	2.474
200,000-499,999	0.895	0.892	0.546	0.657
500,000-999,999	0.187	0.182	0.103	0.124
1,000,000 or more	0.073	0.040	0.051	0.059
Of Which:				
1,000,000-3,999,999	0.0550	0.0293		
4,000,000-6,999,999	0.0128	0.0021		
7,000,000 or more	0.0049	0.0002		
Total	100.0	100.0	100.0	100.0

a. Source: own computations from the 1989 and 1992 SCF.

b. Sources: "Selected Historical and Other Data," *Statistics of Income Bulletin*, Winter 1993-94, Vol. 13, No. 4, pp. 179-80; "Selected Historical and Other Data," *Statistics of Income Bulletin,* Winter 1994-95, Vol. 15, No. 3, pp. 180-81.

The table also compares the size distribution of income computed from the Internal Revenue Service Statistics of Income (SOI) in 1989 and 1992 with that from the two SCF files. The SOI figures are based on actual tax returns filed in the two years. There are three major differences between the two data sources. First, the SOI data use the tax return as the unit of observation, whereas the SCF figures are based on the household unit. Second, individuals who do not file tax returns are excluded from the SOI tabulations. Third, the size distribution for the SOI data is based on adjusted gross income (AGI), whereas the SCF distributions are based on total household income.

Despite the differences in concept and measurement, trends in the size distribution of AGI can give a rough approximation to actual changes in the size distribution of household (Census) income. What is most striking is that the SOI figures show a slight increase in the percent of units in income class $1,000,000 and more, from 0.051 in 1989 to 0.059 percent in 1992, whereas the SCF figures show a sharp decline, from 0.073 to 0.040 percent.

Results from the SOI data fail to provide any independent corroboration for the sharp decline in the number of households with incomes of $1,000,000 or more between 1989 and 1992. Accordingly, I adjusted the 1992 weights so that they are consistent with the 1989 weights—in particular, so that they report the same percentage of households with one million dollars or more of income in the two years.

2. Since average wealth declined in real terms between 1989 and 1992, these calculations could not be performed for this period.

3. Some of the results reported in this section differ somewhat from those reported below, in Table 4-1, for two reasons. First, I base all calculations here on the Survey of Consumer Finances for years 1983, 1989, and 1992. Second, I have used a slightly different division of the population into racial groups.

➢ APPENDIX

1. The inclusion of consumer durables can make a significant difference in estimated wealth concentration. For example, on the basis of the 1983 *Survey of Consumer Finances*, one can calculate a Gini coefficient of 0.80 and a share of wealth held by the top percent, respectively, for HWX.

2. Feldstein (1974).

3. Technically, pension cash surrender value, which is already included in the calculation of HW, is then subtracted from this total to avoid double-counting.

4. Technical details on the estimation of retirement wealth can be found in Feldstein 91974, 1976) and Wolff (1987b, 1988, and 1992).

5. Another set of comparable estimates is also available from the U.S. Census Bureau's 1984 and 1988 Survey of Income and Program Participation (SIPP) data set. However, as suggested later, because the SIPP is a representative sample)and as such tends toward bias in measuring the uppermost echelons of the distribution, as opposed to a stratified sample designed to capture this segment more accurately), the wealth inequality estimates do not appear very reliable. See Wolff (1994) for further details.

6. Lampman (1962).

7. Smith (1984, 1987).

8. Wolff and Marley (1989).

9. For example, in Smith's estimates pensions are included only at their

cash surrender value, and a large percentage of trusts — those that were not directly under the control of the deceased — are measured at their actuarial value since that is how they are measured in the estate files. On the other hand, Lampman used a wealth formula that includes the full value of pensions as well as trusts. Because of the fraction of trusts not included, Smith's reported concentration estimates are biased downward in relation to Lampman's.

10. Goldsmith (1962).

11. Ruggles and Ruggles (1982).

12. Schwartz (1983).

13. See Wolff (1994) for details.

14. Atkinson (1975); Shorrocks (1987).

15. See Wolff and Marley (1989) for details.

16. See Wolff (1987a) and Wolff (1994) for details.

17. See Wolff (1980) and Wolff (1983) for details.

18. Radner and Vaughan (1987).

19. Avery and Kennickell (1994).

20. See Wolff and Marley (1989), Appendix II, for details.

21. Perhaps somewhat coincidentally, the share of total assets and net worth owned by the top 1 percent of *households* in 1962 computed on the basis of the SFCC lines up almost exactly with the share of total assets and net worth owned by the tip 1 percent of *individuals* on the basis of the estate tax data. The same relation holds for 1969.

22. According to the original figures of Smith (1987), the share of net worth owned by the top 1 percent of wealth holders fell from 27.7 percent in 1972 to 19.2 percent in 1976. Schwartz (1984-85) reported a slightly higher share of net worth owned by the top percentile in 1976, 20.8 percent; Table A-1uses Schwartz's figure rather than Smith's for the "New Series" in column 6.

23. See Smith (1987).

24. This trend is confirmed in more recent estate tax figures. According to Schwartz (1984-85), the share of total personal wealth held by the top 2.8 percent of the nation's adult population was 28 percent in 1982, and, according to Schwartz amd Kpjmspm (1990), the share held by the top 1.6 percent of the adult population was 28.5 percent in 1986.

25. See Wolff and Marley (1989) for details.

26. See Wolff(1987b) and Wolff and Marley (1989) for details.

27. The estimates shown here are based on the assumption that real average Social Security benefits grow by 2 percent per year over time.

28. In the United Kingdom, the threshold is considerably lower, so that the vast majority of estates file tax returns.

29. Estate tax data have been extensively used by Atkinson and

Harrison (1978) and Shorrocks (1987) for the United Kingdom; and Lampman (1962), Smith (1974, 1984, 1987), Smith and Franklin (1974), and Wolff and Marley (1989) for the United States. The long-term time-series concentration estimates for Britain and the United States are based on estate tax data and the individual unit of account.

30. See U.S. Bureau of the Census (1986 and 1990a) for details.

31. These are the 1962 *survey of Financial Characteristics of Consumers*—see Projector and Weiss (1966) for a description the 1983 *survey of Consumer Finances*—see Kennickell and Shack-Marquez (1992) for a description. The 1992 *Survey of Consumer Finances* is also in the works but has not been released yet.

32. It is unlikely that the differences in results can be accounted for by the difference in years, since the discrepancies are large between the 1983 SCF and 1984 SIPP *as well as* between the 1988 SIPP and the 1989 SCF.

33. See Wolff (1994) for more details.

34. Spant (1987).

35. Stewart (1939).

36. Wolff (1980, 1982, and 1983).

37. Greenwood (1983, 1987).

BIBLIOGRAPHY

Atkinson, A. B. "The Distribution of Wealth in Britain in the 1960's: The Estate Duty Method Reexamined." In James D. Smith, ed., *The Personal Distribution of Income and Wealth*, Studies in Income and Wealth, vol. 39 (New York: National Bureau of Economic Research, 1975).

Atkinson, A. B., and A. J. Harrison. *Distribution of Personal Wealth in Britain.* (Cambridge: Cambridge University Press, 1978).

Avery, Robert B., and Arthur B. Kennickell. "U.S. Household Wealth: Changes from 1983 to 1986." In Edward N. Wolff, ed., *Research in Economic Inequality*, vol. 4 (Greenwich, Conn.: JAI Press, 1993).

Avery, Robert B., Gregory E. Elliehausen, Glenn B. Canner, and Thomas A. Gustafson. "Survey of Consumer Finances, 1983." Board of Governors of the Federal Reserve System, *Federal Reserve Bulletin* 70, no. 3 (September 1984): 679–92.

Board of Governors of the Federal Reserve System. *Survey of Financial Characteristics of Consumers.* Washington, D.C., 1962. Database.

Board·of Governors of the Federal Reserve System. *Survey of Consumer Finances* Washington, D.C., 1983, 1986, and 1989. Databases.

Board of Inland Revenue (United Kingdom). *Inland Revenue Statistics, 1992.* (London: Her Majesty's Statistical Office, 1992).

David, Martin. "Increased Taxation with Increased Acceptability: A Discussion of Net Worth Taxation as a Federal Revenue Alternative." *Journal of Finance* 28, no. 2 (May 1973): 481–95.

Feldstein, Martin. "Social Security, Induced Retirement, and Aggregate Capital Accumulation." *Journal of Political Economy* 82, no. 5 (September/October 1974): 905–26.

—. "Social Security and the Distribution of Wealth." *Journal of the American Statistical Association* 71, no. 356 (December 1976): 800–807.

Goldsmith, Raymond W. *The National Wealth of the United States in the Postwar Period*, National Bureau of Economic Research. (Princeton, N.J.: Princeton University Press, 1962).

Greenwood, Daphne T. "An Estimation of U.S. Family Wealth and Its Distribution from Microdata, 1973." *Review of Income and Wealth*, series 29, no. 1 (March 1983): 23–43.

—. "Age, Income, and Household Size: Their Relation to Wealth Distribution in the United States." In E. Wolff, ed., *International Comparisons of the Distribution of Household Wealth* (New York: Oxford University Press, 1987), pp. 121–40.

Greenwood, Daphne T., and Edward N. Wolff. "Changes in Wealth in the United States, 1962–1983: Savings, Capital Gains, Inheritance, and Lifetime Transfers." *Journal of Population Economics* 5, no. 4 (1992): 261–88.

Kennickell, A. B., and J. Shack-Marquez. "Changes in Family Finances from 1983 to 1989: Evidence from the Survey of Consumer Finances." Board of Governors of the Federal Reserve System, *Federal Reserve Bulletin* 78, no. 1 (January 1992): 1–18.

Kessler, Denis, and Edward N. Wolff. "A Comparative Analysis of Household Wealth Patterns in France and the United States." *Review of Income and Wealth*, series 37, no. 3 (September 1991): 249–66.

Kuznets, Simon. *Shares of Upper Income Groups in Income and Savings*. (New York: National Bureau of Economic Research, 1953).

Lampman, Robert. *The Share of Top Wealth-Holders in National Wealth, 1922–56*. (Princeton, N.J.: Princeton University Press, 1962).

Levy, Frank, and Richard Murnane. "Earnings Levels and Earnings Inequality." *Journal of Economic Literature* 30, no. 3 (September 1992): 1331–81.

Modigliani, Franco, and Richard Brumberg. "Utility Analysis and the Consumption Function: An Interpretation of Cross-Section Data." In K. Kurihara, ed., *Post-Keynesian Economics* (New Brunswick, N.J.: Rutgers University Press, 1954).

O'Higgins, Michael, Guenther Schmaus, and Geoffrey Stephenson. "Income Distribution and Redistribution: A Microdata Analysis for Seven Countries." *Review of Income and Wealth*, series 35, no. 2 (June 1989): 107–32.

Organization for Economic Cooperation and Development. *Taxation of Net Wealth, Capital Transfers and Capital Gains of Individuals*. (Paris: OECD, 1988).

Organization for Economic Cooperation and Development. *National Accounts, Detailed Tables, 1978–1990*, vol. 2. (Paris: OECD, 1992).

Pechman, Joseph A. *Who Paid the Taxes, 1966–1985?*. (Washington, D.C.: The Brookings Institution, 1985).

Projector, Dorothy, and Gertrude Weiss. *Survey of Financial Charactersitics of Consumers*. Federal Reserve Technical Papers, Board of Governors of the Federal Reserve System, 1966.

Radner, Daniel B., and Denton R. Vaughan. "Wealth, Income, and the Economic Status of Aged Households." In E. Wolff, ed., *International Comparisons of the Distribution of Household Wealth* (New York: Oxford University Press, 1987), pp. 93–120.

Ruggles, Richard, and Nancy Ruggles. "Integrated Economic Accounts for the United States, 1947–1980." *Survey of Current Business* 62, no. 5 (May 1982): 1–53.

Schwartz, Marvin. "Trends in Personal Wealth 1976–1981." Internal Revenue Service, *Statistics of Income Bulletin* 3, no. 1 (Summer 1983): 1–26.

—. "Preliminary Estimates of Personal Wealth, 1982: Composition of Assets." Internal Revenue Service, *Statistics of Income Bulletin* 4, no. 3 (Winter 1984–85): 1–17.

Schwartz, Marvin, and Barry Johnson. "Estimates of Personal Wealth, 1986." Internal Revenue Service, *Statistics of Income Bulletin* 9, no. 4 (Spring 1990): 63–78.

Shorrocks, A. F. "U.K. Wealth Distribution: Current Evidence and Future Prospects." In E. Wolff, ed., *International Comparisons of the Distribution of Household Wealth* (New York: Oxford University Press, 1987), pp. 29–50.

Smith, James D. "The Concentration of Personal Wealth in America, 1969." *Review of Income and Wealth*, series 20, no. 2 (June 1974): 143–80.

—. "Trends in the Concentration of Personal Wealth in the United States, 1958–1976." *Review of Income and Wealth*, series 30, no. 4 (December 1984): 419–28.

—. "Recent Trends in the Distribution of Wealth in the U.S.: Data, Research Problems, and Prospects." In E. Wolff, ed., *International Comparisons of the Distribution of Household Wealth* (New York: Oxford University Press, 1987), pp. 72–89.

Smith, James D., and Stephen Franklin. "The Concentration of Personal Wealth, 1922–1969." *American Economic Review* 64, no. 2 (May 1974): 162–67.

Spånt, Roland. "Wealth Distribution in Sweden: 1920–1983." In E. Wolff, ed., *International Comparisons of the Distribution of Household Wealth* (New York: Oxford University Press, 1987), pp. 51–71.

Statistics Sweden. *Income Distribution Survey in 1990*. (Örebro, Sweden: SCB Publishing Unit, 1992).

Steuerle, C. Eugene. "Realized Income and Wealth for Owners of Closely Held Farms and Businesses: A Comparison." *Public Finance Quarterly* 12 (October 1984): 407–24.

Stewart, Charles. "Income Capitalization as a Method of Estimating the Distribution of Wealth by Size Group." In *Studies in Income and Wealth*, vol. 3 (New York: National Bureau of Economic Research, 1939).

Tait, Alan A. *The Taxation of Personal Wealth.* (Urbana, Ill.: University of Illinois Press, 1967).

U.S. Bureau of the Census. *Current Population Reports*, series P–70, no. 7, "Household Wealth and Asset Ownership, 1984." (Washington, D.C.: U.S. Government Printing Office, 1986).

U.S. Bureau of the Census. *Current Population Reports*, series P–70, no. 22, "Household Wealth and Asset Ownership, 1988." (Washington, D.C.: U.S. Government Printing Office, 1990[a]).

U.S. Bureau of the Census. *Current Population Reports*, series P–60, no. 167, "Trends in Income by Selected Characteristics: 1947–1988." (Washington, D.C.: U.S. Government Printing Office, 1990[b]).

U.S. Bureau of the Census. *Current Population Reports*, series P–60, no. 168, "Money Income and Poverty Status in the United States, 1989." (Washington, D.C.: U.S. Government Printing Office, 1990[c]).

U.S. Bureau of the Census. *Statistical Abstract of the United States, 1991*, 112th ed. (Washington, D.C.: U.S. Government Printing Office, 1991).

U.S. Bureau of the Census. *Survey of Income and Program Participation.* Washington, D.C., 1984, 1989. Databases.

U.S. Council of Economic Advisers. *Economic Report of the President.* (Washington, D.C.: U.S. Government Printing Office, various years).

Wolff, Edward N. "Estimates of the 1969 Size Distribution of Household Wealth in the U.S. from a Synthetic Database." In James D. Smith, ed., *Modeling the Distribution and Intergenerational Transmission of Wealth* (Chicago: University of Chicago Press, 1980).

—. "Effect of Alternative Imputation Techniques on Estimates of Household Wealth in the U.S. in 1969." In D. Kessler, A. Masson, and D. Strauss-Kahn, eds., *Accumulation et Repartition des Patrimoines.* (Paris: Economica, 1982).

—. "The Size Distribution of Household Disposable Wealth in the United States." *Review of Income and Wealth*, series 29, (June 1983): 125–46.

—. "Estimates of Household Wealth Inequality in the U.S., 1962–1983." *Review of Income and Wealth*, series 33, (September 1987[a]): 231–56.

—. "The Effects of Pensions and Social Security on the Distribution of Wealth in the United States." In E. Wolff, ed., *International Comparisons of the Distribution of Household Wealth* (New York: Oxford University Press, 1987[b]): 208–47.

—. "Social Security, Pensions, and the Life Cycle Accumulation of Wealth: Some Empirical Tests." *Annales d'Economie et de Statistique*, no. 9 (January–March 1988): 199–226.

—. "Methodological Issues in the Estimation of Retirement Wealth." In D. Slottje, ed., *Research in Economic Inequality*, vol. 2 (Greenwich, Conn.: JAI Press, 1992), pp. 31–56.

—. "Trends in Household Wealth in the United States during the 1980s." *Review of Income and Wealth*, series 40, no. 2 (June 1994): 143–74.

Wolff, Edward N., and Marcia Marley. "Long-Term Trends in U.S. Wealth Inequality: Methodological Issues and Results." In R. Lipsey and H. Tice, eds., *The Measurement of Saving, Investment, and Wealth*, Studies of Income and Wealth, vol. 52 (Chicago: University of Chicago Press, 1989), pp. 765–839.

INDEX

About the Author

Edward N. Wolff received his Ph.D. from Yale University in 1974 and is currently professor of economics at New York University, where he has taught since 1974. He also serves as managing editor of the *Review of Income and Wealth*, as an associate editor of the *Journal of Population Economics* and *Structural Change and Economic Dynamics*, as a council member of the International Association for Research in Income and Wealth, and on the editorial board of *Economics Systems Research*. His principal research areas are productivity growth and income and wealth distribution. He is the author of *Growth, Accumulation, and Unproductive Activity: An Analysis of the Post-War U.S. Economy* (Cambridge University Press, 1987); a coauthor of *Productivity and American Leadership: The Long View* (MIT Press, 1989), *The Information Economy: The Implications of Unbalanced Growth* (The Institute for Research on Public Policy, 1989), and *Competitiveness, Convergence, and International Specialization* (MIT Press, 1993); the editor of *International Comparisons of the Distribution of Household Wealth* (Oxford University Press, 1987) and volume 4 of *Research in Economic Inequality* (JAI Press, 1993); and a coeditor of *International Perspectives on Profitability and Accumulation* (Edward Elgar Publishing Ltd., 1992), and *Convergence of Productivity: Cross-National Studies and Historical Evidence* (Oxford University Press, 1994). He is also the author of many articles published in books and professional journals.